A New

HUMANITY

A New HUMANITY

A WALK THROUGH THE LETTER OF EPHESIANS

LUCIANO LOMBARDI

A NEW HUMANITY
Copyright © 2023 by Luciano Lombardi
First printing: 2014, Second printing: 2023

ISBN: 978-1-4866-2358-7
eBook ISBN: 978-1-4866-2359-4

Word Alive Press
119 De Baets Street Winnipeg, MB R2J 3R9
www.wordalivepress.ca

WORD ALIVE
—P R E S S—

Cataloguing in Publication information can be obtained from Library and Archives Canada.

CONTENTS

PREFACE

I am humbled by the reach this book has had through its first eight years in print. When I wrote it, my thoughts were that I would be satisfied if just my students read it. Well, not only have my students read it, but so have many friends, colleagues, pastors, and scholars, along with people in the many churches I have visited since this book came out. Several that I have never met were thoughtful enough to send me notes along the way to let me know how the book impacted their faith. Your response and support over these years have encouraged me to continue with the most recent publication of *A Free Humanity: A Walk Through the Letter of Galatians.*

It is reassuring to know that this book will continue through this present imprint to spread the news of our new humanity, which our Lord Jesus has so sacrificially achieved for us. In knowing the extent of the love of the Triune God for our humanity and our world, I pray that so many more will come to know of the depths with which they are loved, cared for, and thought of by Father, Son, and Spirit.

Thanks to the Word Alive Press team who have come alongside to help me keep this book in print and draw a new audience to its pages. Thank you to Debbie Sawczak who contributed her expertise in editing the original manuscript and gave my writing a definite lift in its continuity and scope of meaning. I missed the opportunity to thank her in the first imprint. I am happy to be able to redeem that omission in this edition. Thank you as well to Faithlife for digitizing the book and making it part of an electronic collection. Your partnership ensures that this book will always have a life in the digital world.

As I trust the Lord to do what he wills with these words in these pages, my prayer for you is that you are captured by the reality of the love of the Father, Son, and Spirit in the gift of life that they have given. May you rise to the challenge to live out your faith in kindness, patience, and love as you "put up" with a world that has not yet come of age and still struggles with the bumps and curves that life brings it. May the steps you continue to take in the path of our Lord give you eyes to see what the Spirit sees as the fulfillment of the work of Christ in our world for its redemption and restoration.

Luciano Lombardi
This 16th day of September 2022
Mississauga, Ontario, Canada

INTRODUCTION

This book is an attempt to share a point of view on the Letter to the Ephesians, a point of view that is difficult to find in any published work I have come across. Just today I was reading an Italian commentator who was struggling over the authorship of the letter so as to be able to include it among the Pauline letters in the Bible.[1] My aim is not to enter into such debates, but to take at face value the canonical decision of the first Church Fathers and attribute the writing of Ephesians to Paul the Apostle. Given this premise, my immediate question is, why does Paul write this letter?

The answer comes from a particular traditional argument that runs as follows. While held up in Caesarea Palestine, or under house arrest in Rome, Paul writes a letter to the Colossian church. He is writing to the Colossians to address their reported difficulty in understanding the scope of the divinity of Christ and hence His significance to a believer's view of God. But while waiting for Tychicus to come and pick up the letter and take it to its destination, Paul writes two other letters: Ephesians and Philemon.[2] Philemon is a personal letter to a slave owner, asking him to reconsider taking back his wayward slave, and the Ephesian letter is a general one that Paul intended for the believing community at large. Its goal was to communicate his collective thoughts on God and faith to the various believing communities in Asia Minor. It was an occasion not to focus on any particular problem or issue in a specific church, but rather to communicate to all the believers in the region Paul's big thoughts on God's activity in the world and in the lives of human beings.[3] The mistake then is to regard the original audience of this letter as the Ephesians themselves.

---

[1] Stefano Romanello, *Lettera agli Efesini: I Libri Biblici Nuovo Testamento* (Milano: Figlie di San Paolo, 2003).

[2] Gordon D. Fee and Douglas Stuart, *How to Read the Bible Book by Book: A Guided Tour from Genesis Through to Revelation* (Grand Rapids, MI: Zondervan, 2002), p. 347.

[3] John B. Polhill, *Paul and His Letters* (Nashville, TN: Broadman and Holman, 1999). In chapter 17 Polhill reasons, "Would Paul have written such a general letter to a church where he had worked for nearly three years no more than five years previously, perhaps as recently as two years? Would he need to introduce himself and his ministry …In 3:2 he indicated that they may have 'heard about' his ministry. Would the Ephesians know him only by hearsay?" p. 355.

Scholars who promote a general intent for the letter point out that the earliest manuscript we have for it does not even contain any reference to Ephesus.[4]

Again, my intention is not to argue for this view of the letter's purpose over against other views. Rather, simply assuming this purpose and taking it as a starting point, I intend to show how it shapes our understanding of the letter's message.[5] I leave it to you, the reader, to determine whether the approach I present helps you in your quest to understand Paul the Apostle's view of what God is about in His plan for the world.

What I do know is that I have been presenting this approach to the letter of Ephesians in my Pauline Literature class at Master's College and Seminary for the past decade, with very positive results. The students gain a big-picture view of God's plan and how that plan affects the human race. By tackling this letter first, we enhance our understanding of the other Pauline letters that we cover: the big picture that Paul presents in Ephesians, of Jesus' work in creating *one new humanity*,[6] remains in the forefront as we read the other letters, and is the key to understanding them. I know this may sound to some like a rather gutsy departure from the historical Protestant focus on the letter to the Romans as Paul's seminal theological piece; but I am at the point in my career as a ministry leader, pastor, and Bible college professor where I desire to let the Bible, and so God's Spirit, continually renew my thinking about what it says so that I might come to a greater understanding of our role as followers of Christ. I am prepared to risk sounding biased and one-sided in order to present what I have found to be an eye-opening perspective on this letter.[7] I pray that, by picking up this book

---

[4] Polhill, p. 355: "The reference to Ephesus is lacking in the three earliest manuscript witnesses to Ephesians – papyrus 46, and codexes Vaticanus and Sinaiticus." Cf. G.B. Caird, *Paul's Letters from Prison: Ephesians, Philippians, Colossians, Philemon* (Oxford University Press, 1976), p. 8: "The uniformity of the titles shows that they must have been added by second century scribes after the letters had been collected into a corpus. The only letter which contains nothing to justify its title is Ephesians. For the words 'in Ephesus,' which are found at 1:1 in all later manuscripts, are missing from these early ones, and also from Basil (Adv. Eunom. ii.) an explicit statement, written about A.D. 370, that they were omitted by the oldest authorities known to him."

[5] In this case I'm not attempting a scholarly debate in which several views are analyzed side by side. My aim is to make this presentation accessible to everyone and so offer a single point of view for the purpose of stirring up our thoughts toward an alternative that has helped me and my students tremendously.

[6] ενα καινον ανθρωπον – literally, "one new man." I chose to use "humanity" for ανθρωπον since it has a collective sense including all humanity in chapter 2 of the letter.

[7] N. T. Wright, *Justification* (Downers Grove, IL: IVP Academic, 2009), p. 247: "…if we had begun with Ephesians how different everything would have appeared." Wright comments on the tradition of using Romans, interpreted through the lenses of Protestant Reformers, as a starting place to understand Paul, and how this has obscured Paul's view of Jesus, salvation, righteousness, and justification in relation to the overarching biblical story.

and reading it, you will be challenged to let the Bible renew your thinking in the same way.

Chapter One

THE TRIUNE GOD THAT ADOPTS US

WHAT WOULD YOU WRITE?

If you knew that you were nearing the end of your life, what would you write to those that you would be leaving behind? In our present age of email, texting, Facebook messaging, and twittering, the challenge is to concentrate on writing words that communicate anything of substance, let alone words that express our final thoughts on life, love, relationships, marriage, God, faith, and even death itself. We don't usually communicate with anything like that kind of depth. We use icons, emoticons, acronyms, and texting. Given the challenge, though, I think all of us would feel the weight of such a task and forgo the idle chitchat we indulge in daily in favour of words that express a lifetime of experience and relationship. I don't think we would waste time commenting on the weather, bringing up petty arguments of the past, or describing our favourite movie of all time.

Given such an important task, I think all of us would seriously consider what the first few words and sentences should be, since these would draw our readers into the last thoughts that we would ever share with the people in our life. That's the sense of urgency and importance Paul experiences as he sets about writing the letter we now call Ephesians. Having written two previous letters, Paul waits for Tychicus to come and carry them to their destination. And as he waits, he writes a third letter that will be the final expression of his thoughts on God, Jesus, humanity, the world, faith, community, and the battle against evil.

I'm going to suggest an idea that I have not heard from many others so far: this letter is Paul's personal manifesto[8] setting out what it means to be a follower of Christ and how God's plan works itself out in the world and in the human race. It is here in this letter that Paul takes the freedom to write large thoughts on God's plan for the world. If what I'm suggesting is true, then we need to pay close attention to the very first words that Paul writes here, since this will show

---

[8] Ibid., p. 43: "Suppose we conduct a thought experiment. Suppose we come to Ephesians first, with Colossians close behind, and decide that we will read Romans, Galatians and the rest in the light of them instead of the other way around. What we will find, straight off, is nothing short of a (very Jewish) cosmic soteriology."

us what he considers to be the necessary starting place when speaking of God's plan and its implications for us and our world.

Ephesians 1:3-6

Blessed be the God and Father of our Lord Jesus Christ, who has blessed us with every Spiritual[9] blessing in the heavenly realms in Christ, choosing us in Christ before the foundation of the world was put in place to be holy and blameless in His sight. He lovingly planned beforehand our adoption through Jesus Christ in keeping with His own pleasure found in the fame of His glorious grace which He freely gives from His loving relationship.[10]

PRESENTING A DISTINCT VIEW OF GOD

Paul presents God as the Philanthropist of the universe: out of the riches of His being, He gives the human race *"every Spiritual blessing in the heavenly realms."* What we have here from Paul is a form of blessing reminiscent of the "traditional Jewish 'blessing' of God."[11] Israel lived in the awareness of a God who engaged in relationship with them and established His presence with them. He was both Father and Ruler of His people. Paul expands this known relationship to include both Jews and Gentiles as recipients of its blessings. What humanity receives as the fruit of this relationship is nothing short of God Himself and His involvement in our life. Everything else that is given both materially and relationally stems from God giving Himself to us.

This is certainly not the picture of a God who demands that his holiness be preserved through the payment of guilt by those who have affronted Him in

---

[9] I take the view of Gordon D. Fee in his book *God's Empowering Presence* (Peabody, MA: Hendrickson, 1994), p. 665, where he emphasizes that when using πνευμα/πνευματικος Paul is almost always referencing the Spirit or the influence of the Spirit. Fee asserts that, in this passage, the Father is said to give not "things", but *Himself* through His Spirit. It is a gift of connection with Him. He notes the embedded Trinitarian framework in these first verses of Ephesians as well as throughout the letter.

[10] I am using my own translation for the purposes of this presentation. I have enclosed in square brackets any words that I have added in order to make the translation read more smoothly or to make explicit what I believe Paul implies.

[11] Gordon D. Fee, *God's Empowering Presence*, p. 664. Fee points out that Paul writes the same type of blessing at the beginning of 2 Corinthians. What is striking in both letters is the focus on God and His character as the foundation for understanding how He relates to humanity and creation. Specifically, what God gives to humanity is indicative of the kind of God that He is. In this case, we see that He is a highly relational God who is known as Father and has given people His own Spirit and the fruit of what He has accomplished for humanity.

every wrong action.[12] Paul doesn't start with an austere, distant, and faceless Being who is displeased with His creation; rather, the portrait he paints is of a Father who lovingly marks out beforehand how His children will survive the attempt of evil to undermine His house and family.[13] From the outset, Paul identifies God's aim as ensuring that humanity is in relationship with Him, and shows how God acts in the person of Jesus to accomplish this, connecting humanity to Him forever. Paul immediately identifies Jesus as the Christ, which is the Greek title equivalent to 'Messiah', and so as the Saviour of humanity anticipated in the Old Testament and the story of Israel. Thus he affirms that Jesus is the culmination of God's plan, revealed to Israel and now solidified in Him. As N. T. Wright puts it:

> Paul's view of the cataclysmic irruption of God into the history of Israel and the world in and through the death and resurrection of Jesus the Messiah was that this heart-stopping, show-stopping, chart-topping moment was, despite initial appearances, and certainly despite Paul's own earlier expectations and initial understanding, the very thing for which the entire history of Israel under Torah and Moses onward, and indeed the entire history of humanity from Adam onward, had been waiting. It is central to Paul that God had a single plan all along through which he intended to rescue the world and the human race, and that this single plan was centered upon the call of Israel, a call which Paul saw coming to fruition in Israel's representative, the Messiah.[14]

All this was a prior decision by God. Before the world's creation, God anticipates both the creatures who will have the capacity to know and enjoy Him and the events that will undermine this relationship. In the true character of Father, He crafts a plan that in Christ the Messiah, the human race and the rest

---

[12] I have long been convinced by scholars such as Colin Gunton, the Torrances (T.F., James, and Allan), N. T. Wright, and friends such as Baxter Kruger and Rikk Watts, that the understanding of God's holiness that was adopted in the Middle Ages, and that gave rise to the penal substitutionary theory of the atonement, was a grave departure from the Trinitarian focus on the God of grace that prevailed during the first few centuries of the church. The latter is represented by Athanasius, Irenaeus of Lyons, and Cyril of Alexandria. The early church was fresh on the heels of Jesus' presentation of the Father as a benevolent Being who loves His creation and desires to free it from evil and renew it in relationship to Him.

[13] We can justifiably assume that behind these statements lies an awareness in Paul of the significance of the Creation story told in Genesis. God creates out of sheer will and pleasure, birthing the plan for the Creation out of a heart of love and out of a desire that other beings might exist with the capacity to experience the beauty and love of the Triune life of God.

[14] N. T. Wright, *Justification*, p. 35.

of creation will be rescued from the advance of evil. This gives a certain coherence to the construction of Paul's letter: he starts out by describing the nature of God's action at the beginning of humanity's story, and finishes off the letter by indicating how humanity, in the form of God's community, will join God in continuing to carry out His plan.

In the same way, Paul intentionally mentions the "heavenly places" at the beginning, making it clear who rules there and what good comes from there, because he will pick this up again at the end of the letter when he writes about spiritual warfare; in 6:12, Paul also mentions the heavenly places, but there he speaks of the evil forces that lurk in that realm, bent on perpetuating evil. Overall in the letter, he confirms the existence of two powers in the heavenly realms: one is the Father who lavishes Spiritual blessings on humanity, along with His Son the Messiah who will deliver humanity from evil; the other is the evil one and his hordes bent on destroying humanity. Paul is clear about who is the stronger of the two, and how the Father has put in motion a plan that will rescue the world and humanity from the hands of evil.[15]

Paul wants to leave no doubt in his readers' minds as to who the God of the Jewish people is and what He has done to secure relationship with humanity. But the God and Father of the Jewish people is also the God and Father of the Gentiles! This Father holds nothing back: all that is His is given to His Son and so shared with the human race. Our relationship with Him has been settled in His heart before time and creation. He loved us before we ever existed, and, knowing what evil would do to his creation, laid out a plan to ensure that our relationship with Him would remain intact: *holy* and *blameless* are terms that carry a notion of unbroken relationship. Our lives are solidified forever in the person of Christ, who permits nothing to separate us from His love (thus *holiness*) and no action of ours to sabotage His philanthropy (thus *blameless*). These two characteristics of our standing with God the Father are secured through the person of Jesus the Messiah. The two terms are relational terms that identify the status of our relationship to God through the work of Christ in us.[16]

---

[15] Gordon D. Fee, *God's Empowering Presence*, p. 723. "The 'powers' have been a concern from the opening words of the *berakah* in 1:3, where the blessings associated with the Spirit belong to God's people 'in the heavenlies,' in the habitation of the 'powers.' The reasons for his recipients' being able to experience such blessings, 'in the heavenlies,' are then spelled out in a variety of ways throughout."

[16] This underlines the view of Paul that I believe best illuminates the meaning of what he writes regarding our relationship with God and what God accomplishes for us through Christ. Other scholars will focus on the terms *holy* and *blameless* to reference an "imputed righteousness" that effects substantive change to our being through a transfer from Christ to us. Such a view assumes that Paul is using Greek philosophical categories, where being is understood in terms of substance,

Think of it personally for a moment. Our true beginning as human beings is in the heart of God our Father, the One who gives us life. It was His desire to create us so that we might be in relationship with Him and live out that relationship through connection to the Divine community of Father, Son, and Spirit. He knows that evil will undermine this purpose, but creates anyway—not so that humanity might suffer, but so that humanity will ultimately have the pleasure of knowing Him. Before anything happens, He ensures that His plan will prevail and confirm our restoration to Him. Paul will refer to this rescue and restoration as adoption.

THE PRIMARY CONCEPT OF SALVATION IS ADOPTION

Paul then introduces the concept of adoption. Bear with me for a moment as I retrace his logic at this point in the letter. If this letter is a general letter to all believers in Asia Minor, in which Paul takes the opportunity to unfold what he believes to be God's plan for the Creation, then the mention of adoption by Paul in this introductory description is not an arbitrary choice of words but a careful, intentional step in his presentation. For centuries Protestants have touted justification as the main theological theme in Paul.[17] But if that were so, then given the important scope of this letter, one would think that justification would feature among the first words and concepts presented in such a general address.[18]

---

as opposed to Hebrew relational categories that describe God's connection, in His own presence and action, to humanity and creation. Paul's writings make far more sense when he is considered to be thinking as a Hebrew rather than as a Greek.

[17] To be specific, they mean justification in the sense that our sins are forgiven and we are going to heaven. But where Paul does talk about justification, he gives it a narrower meaning related to the greater concept of adoption and hence the fulfillment of covenant promise. See N.T. Wright, *Justification*, pp. 90–91, where he points out that "to justify" does not "denote an action which transforms someone so much as a declaration which grants them a status."

[18] Of course, the Protestant Reformers and their followers also touted Romans as the controlling letter outlining Paul's theological thinking. I disagree. I truly think that Ephesians is the letter giving us the clearest path of Paul's theological thought as to what God is up to in His involvement with Creation. Cf. N.T. Wright, *Justification*, p. 44: "We need to understand doctrines, their statement, development, confutation, restatement and so on, within the multiple social, cultural, political, and of course ecclesial and theological settings of their time." The Reformers looked at Paul through the lens of their own sense of need for a resolution of their personal guilt. In this way they shifted the concept of salvation towards an emphasis on God's forgiveness of the individual. In reality, such forgiveness is a secondary implicate of the greater point Paul makes concerning what Jesus accomplishes for us. This will be seen clearly in chapter 2 of Ephesians.

What Paul does mention here is not justification but *adoption* as the description of God's goal for the human race.[19] This will set the stage for his discussion in chapter 2 of how God gathers up humanity in Christ, in which he expands on the significance of adoption and what it does to humanity. But at this immediate point in chapter 1, adoption is described simply as the loving act of God the Father as He wills, before he creates, that his creation will be reconnected to Him through Christ so that relationship with Him is maintained.[20] Paul speaks of a God who takes *pleasure* in such forethought, and underlines the impact of God's decision on God's own self in terms of His preparedness in Christ for the entire human race to be forever connected to Him.[21]

The gathering of Jews and Gentiles into one new humanity in chapter 2 indicates to me that here in chapter 1, "those He loves" make up the entire human race. This gracious, freely giving God has targeted no less than the human race as the object of His desire for adoption. Think of it! Every human being has been reconnected to God the Father in Christ so as to have a place in God's family. As Protestant Christians we have often considered that because we have come to a place of understanding, and have "accepted Christ", we are part of His family while those in darkness are not. But the meaning of Paul's words regarding God's activity and the scope of its influence is that even those who live in darkness have been adopted.[22]

---

[19] Theologically, the terms *holy* and *blameless* in this passage reference a "declarative" statement that characterizes "justification" as defined by N.T. Wright in fn 15 above, where the pronouncement is that humanity is in "right relationship" with God. This is all the more remarkable when humanity has not been created yet; the anticipation of God in providing for His creation shows His loving character. But as can be clearly seen, that is specifically to serve the grand purpose of "adoption" outlined in this verse.

[20] This is none other than the Jewish view of God's plan for Israel, expanded by Paul to include the Gentiles as well in light of the revelation of Jesus. Paul will find ample evidence of this in the Old Testament, where God defines Israel's role as the people through whom He will make his name known among the nations—the Father who gives every Spiritual blessing in the heavenly realms!

[21] At this point some of you may say, "This is beginning to sound like universalism." The choice I make is to take Paul at his word. I have not adopted the Calvinist approach to this passage, as I think it not only distracts from Paul's words but also inaccurately identifies the target of God's loving actions. Paul is clearly speaking of God choosing the entire human race to be recovered in Christ and to experience adoption. We will see that, later on in the letter, Paul indicates that each human being has the choice either to live in the *light* of such relationship or to live in the *darkness* unaware of such a connection.

[22] Again, I anticipate the insistence by some that those in darkness are lost; but the reality is that they too have been given such free grace and love from God. We will see that later in Ephesians Paul describes those in darkness as being in a state of "sleep", completely unaware that they are part of a cosmic relationship that includes them in God's community. Living in such darkness can be quite sinister, as Paul will describe early on in chapter 2.

To consider any other alternative betrays the very intent of God in His cosmic plan. If those He loves are specific people, already picked out beforehand over against others, then this is not lavish grace that Paul is speaking of but rather preferential, selective grace.[23] I truly believe there is no point in pursuing this line of interpretation in Paul, since it is contrary to his clear mission of preaching the Good News, and the indication by supporting biblical authors (such as Luke) that the mission of the early church was to evangelize the Roman Empire.[24] I have used the phrase "from His loving relationship" to translate Paul's literal "in the Beloved" in order to clarify what he is referring to with this prepositional phrase. He is pointing out that the grace of God, coming to humanity through Christ, is the fruit of the loving relationship that exists between the Father and the Son. The love of God for humanity through Christ is nothing short of the expression of the Father's loving relationship with the Son, spilling over to the creation![25] This love has no limits. We will see that Paul quickly brings the Spirit into the equation as well, as the One who seals all of this in terms of its realization in the human race.

Keeping in mind the political climate of the day, it is interesting to note that the Roman Emperor declared himself the "Father" of the Empire. The desire of these Roman rulers was to gather all nations under the Fatherhood of the Empire so that all could benefit from the riches of Rome lavished upon its citizens.[26]

---

[23] In 6:9, Paul will make it clear that God has no such bias of one person or group over another. Israel makes this mistake, assuming that they are the preferred people of God over against the Gentiles, but Paul will squash this thought rather quickly in chapter 2.

[24] This is why I refuse to translate προορίσας as "predestination." The Calvinistic attachments to this word completely distort the intent of Paul in identifying God as the Philanthropist who lavishly gives the human race His love and acceptance through Christ. It is a much more relational language that Paul is using, building on the Old Testament view of God as the eternal Father of the nation of Israel and so of the human race. The notion Paul is getting across is not one of philosophical determinism but of a fatherly act of providence. For a commentary on the cosmic evangelistic perspective of the early church, see John Stott's commentary on Acts, *The Spirit, The Church and the World* (Downer's Grove, IL: IVP, 1990).

[25] See G.B. Caird, *Paul's Letters from Prison*, p. 36: "But the title [Beloved] is used here to indicate that the bounty God lavishes on men consists in their being caught up into the love which subsists between Father and Son (cp. John 17:23, 26)."

[26] Richard Gordon, in his article "The Veil of Power" in *Paul and Empire: Religion and Power in Roman Imperial Society*, ed. by Richard Horsley (Harrisburg, PA: Trinity Press International, 1997), speaks of the unity the Emperor brought to religious aspects of Roman life (specifically in taking on the role of Priest and Sacrificer) including the title of "regulator of the world and **father** of the earth" (p. 129). The historian Suetonius in his account *The Twelve Caesars* (Harmondsworth, UK: Penguin, 1957) describes how this fatherhood of the Empire passed by tradition from one emperor to the other. Whether they truly believed it at heart or not, the emperors used it as propaganda in attempting to unite the Empire.

Those in leadership enjoyed the privileged status and high regard of benefactors to the Empire, when in reality they were benefiting themselves above all.[27] Given such a scenario, Paul's description of God as the Father of the human race, who lavishes the gifts of His kingdom on humanity, contrasts vividly with the track record of the Emperors in carrying out their "fatherly" task. Paul's message about God's providential love overshadows the broken promises made by Roman rulers.

Ephesians 1:7-14[28]

We have been redeemed by the blood of Christ, our wrong ways cancelled out because of His rich grace that He has heaped on us. Out of His wisdom and knowledge comes His great pleasure to make known to us the secret of His plan which is leading toward the completion of the setting of all things in heaven and on earth under the leadership of Christ. In Him we have been given an inheritance that the Father planned for beforehand according to the working out of His eternal plan. And we who have come to hope in Christ give tribute to such a glorious future. Believing in the truth of such good news of our salvation, the Holy Spirit has sealed this promise to us, He being the guarantee of our inheritance until it comes to be vested fully in us.

GOD'S PLAN CENTRED ON CHRIST

On the heels of having conveyed to his readers the astonishing philanthropy of the Father in His adoption of the human race through Jesus Christ, Paul introduces the significance of the sacrifice of Jesus for the human race as the object of this lavish grace. The shedding of the blood of Jesus on the cross is not understood as payment demanded by a holy God who feels His character and honour besmirched by humanity's sin and must be appeased. Rather, it is presented under the metaphor of redemption, echoing the language of Israel's story in Exodus where God frees His people from bondage in Egypt.[29] Paul tells the story of this same loving God, the Father of the whole human race, focused on an even grander rescue: God prepares a plan to rescue all humanity from the evil

---

[27] Richard Horsley, ed., *Paul and Empire*, pp. 18–19: "Augustus's restoration of the commonwealth, reinforced by the supposed revival of traditional virtues and religion, however, involved deep-running contradictions …simply reinforced the power of the wealthy landowners at the expense of the Italian peasantry indebted from fighting the battles of their warlord creditors."

[28] I have chosen to divide verses 3–14 into two sections so as to make my commentary on this section manageable, but in reality Paul writes these verses as one continuous sentence. So powerful are these thoughts that there is absolutely no pause in Paul's writing of them. Paul does do this elsewhere, but not quite to the same degree as in this letter with this passage.

[29] See G.B. Caird, *Paul's Letters from Prison*, p. 37.

undermining it, through Christ's sacrifice, which cancels out the consequences of life lived apart from and out of relationship with the philanthropic God of the universe. All the wrong paths that humanity has taken in light of being misled by evil are cancelled through the life and sacrifice of Jesus. All the tension, hatred, animosity, and dysfunction lived out by the human race, men and women against men and women, is cancelled out by the life and death of Jesus.

The idea expressed by "cancelled" has the concept of stoppage embedded in it.[30] Whatever evil element entered the human race at the fall has now been stopped; it no longer has the power to gain any ground in the human race. Jesus, by the giving of His life including His birth, ministry, death, resurrection, and ascension, has pronounced a great "NO"[31] to any continuation of evil perpetuating the waywardness of the human race. In Christ, God has brought the human race under the lordship of the King of heaven. In fact, astonishingly, God's plan brings *everything* under such lordship. As Paul mentions in Colossians, all rulers, powers, principalities, people, heaven, earth, creation—literally all things—are under the headship of Christ, ruled by the values of God's kingdom, each person and thing assigned its true value, dignity, identity, and purpose.[32] This is essentially the "inheritance" that Paul speaks about in these verses. We are inheriting our lives, which in their final vesting will be free of evil altogether. The forgiveness, or, as I have translated it in this portion of the letter, *cancellation* of our waywardness will be realized in its fullness at the end when God completes the ordering of the world under Christ.[33]

---

[30] See Colin Brown, *The New International Dictionary of New Testament Theology: Volume 1* (Grand Rapids, MI: Zondervan, 1975), pp. 697–702. In particular the function of αφεσις is forgiveness that enables the recipient to experience μετανοια, a change in perspective. The act of forgiveness causes people to view God and themselves in a different light – viewing the "old humanity" as dead. Paul will of course engage this point later in the letter, in chapter 2 and in chapters 4 and 5.

[31] See Karl Barth in his commentary on Romans concerning the reality that it is God who says "NO" to sin in the human race and "YES" to grace; it is something God does in us through Christ and does not exist in any "concrete fashion" in the human race. Karl Barth, *The Epistle to the Romans*, 6th ed., translated by Edwin C. Hoskyns (London: Oxford University Press, 1968), p. 213.

[32] In the Ephesian letter Paul chooses to focus on the gathering of all humanity under Christ's lordship, but not so as to ignore the rest of Creation. Paul's point in this letter is to speak specifically on what God's secret plan has accomplished for the human race, as a far superior alternative to the vain promise held out by the cult of the Roman Emperor to gather all people under the Emperor's headship in order to establish peace and prosperity. Read Suetonius' biographies of the twelve Caesars for descriptions of such visions during the early church era. The Ephesian letter runs counter to the culture of the "Babylon" of the day and its own claims to power and rule.

[33] In a chapel address at Wheaton College, you can hear N.T. Wright brilliantly begin his talk on Ephesians by outlining how, in 1:10, God's plan comes to reality in the gathering up of all things in Christ. The talk was given Friday, April 16, 2010 as part of the 19th Annual Wheaton Theology Conference.

Paul then offers two assurances of the reality of this plan of God for humanity. The first is that those who have already come to believe in Christ and his lordship exemplify a living hope in the glorious future that God is bringing to His Creation; that is, the presence of believers right now is evidence of God's plan being fulfilled. The second is the presence of the Holy Spirit as a seal or sign indicating that the inheritance will come in its fullness. As this community continues to exist, the Spirit, working now in them and now through them, will be a formidable force in the Creation with the goal of completely saturating it with God's presence in the person of Christ. The ultimate consummation will be heaven on earth.[34]

THE SPIRIT AS THE GUARANTEE

This statement by Paul gives us insight into his understanding of the Spirit's role in God's secret plan. Paul is building on the familiar biblical vision of God restoring Creation to its connection with Him, as found in prophetic voices such as Ezekiel's.[35] The Spirit's activity in the already-established community of believers is evidence of God reaching back from the future into the present. The person of the Trinity who has hovered over the earth from the beginning, who was present in the work of Creation then, continues to be present in its ongoing renewal, realized in part now out of the breadth of its full realization in the end.[36] Paul sees the Spirit reaching out of the fullness of His own relationship with the Father and Son towards us in our present relationship with Christ. The relationship enjoyed by the Trinity (Father, Son, and Spirit), a relationship of mutual indwelling, involvement, and acceptance, of love and embrace, is revealed to us by the Spirit's presence right now among the community of believers. Although already available to us now, participation in the Triune life

---

[34] Jesus taught the disciples to pray for such an outcome. The entire biblical narrative is an unfolding of the story of God restoring relationship with humanity on earth.

[35] We can be reasonably confident that the New Testament writers built on the vision delivered to Israel in Ezekiel 36, of God cleansing Israel as a people and putting His Spirit in them so that they are able to keep His commands. It is in this and similar prophecies that scholars such as Gordon Fee see the foundation for a full-blown understanding of the Spirit's involvement in the life of humanity as found in the New Testament.

[36] Calvin in his Institutes clearly states that the Spirit is the one who makes efficacious the work of Christ in the believer. At the beginning of Book III, where he speaks of "The Benefits of Christ made available to us by the Secret Operation of the Spirit", Calvin lists the first title of the Spirit as the "Spirit of Adoption" who effects Christ's work of grace through which the Father has embraced the believer. It is this work of the Spirit that causes us to be "Sons of God". John Calvin, *Institutes of the Christian Religion*, trans. by Henry Beveridge (Grand Rapids, MI: Eerdmans, 1993), 3.3.1, p. 464.

of God will be experienced in its fullness in the end, as the inheritance of our adoption outlined by Paul earlier in the chapter.[37]

In these first 14 verses of the letter, Paul outlines none other than the full involvement of Father, Son, and Spirit in the adoption of the human race. This adoption is the inclusion of the human race in relationship with the Father, Son, and Spirit. Once there was alienation, but now there is fellowship. The Spirit's ongoing presence is a continual reminder to us that God's act of adoption will be brought to its fullness in the end. What we have to look forward to is a world where all things are ordered under Christ, everything on earth and in the human race operating under the values of the Kingdom established with the reign of Christ. In this sense Paul's introduction to the letter is also significantly eschatological.

It is difficult for us to picture a world where evil is no longer present, where humanity is restored to full relationship with God, and where the earth no longer suffers under the strain of sin perpetuated in the social context of the human race.[38] Evil is still present, and we witness the effect of evil on our world. But Paul looks to the final goal of God's plan, where evil is no more and where all is made right. Everything in the present is oriented according to what God desires to accomplish in the future. As followers of Christ and communities of believers, we live in the fallen present, with the reality of redemption already at work in us, and the hope of its future consummation as our orientation for living right now. In the next section of the letter, Paul will explain how the Spirit acts continuously in the present to transform the hearts and minds of individuals as the work of Christ for humanity takes shape in those who have now believed.

---

[37] Paul will stipulate later that God's battle with evil is not yet finished. We will join God in his battle to purge evil from the world, and our perseverance over time will be essential to our participation in God's plan. Jump ahead to chapter 6 if you want to see the image Paul draws. The letter brilliantly builds toward this last chapter.

[38] Colin Gunton, *The Christian Faith: An Introduction to Christian Doctrine* (Oxford: Blackwell, 2002), p. 61. Gunton points out that the reason Jesus enters the social context of humanity is to stop the perpetuation of sin within that social context by living his life in representation of the human race, dying to sin and so freeing the human race from it.

Chapter Two

BEING CHANGED FROM THE INSIDE OUT

Ephesians 1:15–23

Having heard of your trust in the Lord Jesus and your love for all the holy ones, I haven't stopped giving thanks for you, remembering you in my prayers. I pray continually that the God of our Lord Jesus, the Father who is famous for grace,[39] give you the Spirit of wisdom and revelation that comes from knowing Him, so that the eyes of your mind are opened to knowing the hope of his calling and knowing the richness of His glorious inheritance that is experienced in His community.[40] I want you to know the immeasurable greatness of His power in His community, exemplified in His raising Jesus from the dead and seating Him at the right hand far above any other ruler, authority, power, or kingdom or any other great name either mentioned in the past or to be honoured in the future. All things are subject to Him and He is ruler over everything for those who gather in His name; His community, His body, filling all things everywhere.

A CHANGE THAT REVEALS A NEW COMMUNITY

Some argue that the commendation by Paul of his readers' trust in God and love for others was addressed specifically to a certain group he had in mind. Although many scholars view this letter as addressed to believers in Ephesus, my view that it is a more general letter, written for believers at large, does not mean that Paul can't commend a larger group of people just as he would a more specific

---

[39] I've chosen to translate δοξης, meaning "glory", by the phrase "famous for grace". The word "glory" continually produces puzzled faces among my students. They do not truly understand the weight and content of this term when applied to God, so I have translated the essence of it into a phrase that they can understand. I know that in the process I risk over-interpreting Paul, but I've done my best to preserve his original meaning and intent by this description of God the Father's character.

[40] The actual final prepositional phrase is "in the saints", but I chose to translate it as "in His community", since Paul is talking about the result of a change in worldview on the part of God's community collectively, i.e., the saints, because of the wisdom and revelation given by the Spirit to understand and experience what God has given to the human race. Eugene Peterson, in his translation *The Message*, translates verse 18 in the following manner: "your eyes focused and clear, so that you can see exactly what it is he is calling you to do, *grasp the immensity of this glorious way of life he has for Christians*" [emphasis mine].

group of people.[41] Paul is typically quick to commend all his readers for their trust in Christ and love for others in the context of a cultural environment in which the authority of rulers was a licence to mistreat others, and ordinary human life was devalued and degraded. The Roman world was a brutal one where only the privileged few received the respect of citizens of the Empire. The majority were slaves who did the bidding of those who owned them, and were treated for the most part as second-class and disposable. As we have seen, authority from God's perspective is very different. God does not drain the life out of us as He goes about being God; on the contrary, he gives life to us. As Father and Ruler of all, He is famous for His gracious giving rather than for extensive conquering and looting.[42]

Paul's attention now shifts to how the Spirit works inside us to reveal to us a way of looking at the world in keeping with our adoption into relationship with the Father, Son, and Spirit. Our relationship with the Father produces wisdom by revealing to us what it means to live in the strength of the renewed life that He gives through Jesus. Having formerly viewed life and the world through lenses that distorted reality,[43] now in relationship with the Trinity we have a reoriented perspective and see all things with new lenses. From this new perspective we recognize our calling as sons and daughters of God, constituting a community that lives together in continuous anticipation of how the power of the life, death, resurrection, and ascension of Jesus will be expressed by the Spirit in our lives and in the world to fulfill all that God wants to give us as His creation. I call this community "God's Community".[44]

What we have here is nothing less than God revealing to us the big picture of what He is up to in our world. What we could never know on our own, God has now revealed to us. Unlike the emperors who continually rebuilt Rome with new

---

[41] John Stott, in *The Message of Ephesians*, p. 53, writes: "Every Christian both believes and loves. It is impossible to be in Christ and not to find oneself drawn both to him in trust and to his people in love (to *all* of them too, in this case Jews and Gentiles without distinction)."

[42] Emperors and generals in the Roman Empire sought after the coveted triumphal entry, in which they were given a hero's welcome and honoured for their achievements. As they entered the city, behind them came their spoils of war in the form of both plundered goods and conquered people. Julius Caesar actually considered trading a year in the position of Consul of the Empire (basically that of commander-in-chief, granted by the Senators) for the "glory" of a triumphal procession and a triumphal arch built in his honour.

[43] Paul will describe exactly what this tainted view is like in the beginning of chapter 2. Its effect is to strip us of any true life lived in harmony with God, others, and creation. With a tainted, sinful view of life, we follow the very base pleasures of our flesh and walk around as if the lights are on when in reality there is nothing inside.

[44] We have altered the meaning of εκκλεσια so that we have lost the sense of what the "church" is. For clarity and to prevent confusion, I will refer to εκκλεσια as "God's community."

palaces and monuments as a testament to the greatness of the Empire and the difference made by their leadership,[45] God dives deep into the heart of humanity to reveal the secrets of His plan to renew the human race and the world. The emperors tried to drive evil out of the Empire by war;[46] God drives evil out of the human race by flooding the human mind and heart with knowledge of His character, His ways, and His purpose. Such a revelation changes our perspective. We see ourselves, others, God, and the world differently: we see everything in keeping with God's promise to purge the world of evil, and we live knowing that evil no longer has a place in our lives because the ruler is none other than King Jesus – to whom no palace or monument dedicated to any other ruler, power, authority, or kingdom could ever compare.[47]

We tend to try and change ourselves by rearranging our lives on the outside. An unsettled feeling about how our life is going causes us to make changes on the outside – our situation, relationships, and surroundings – with the hope that we will come to have a different perspective on the inside. All too often, however, we end up feeling empty after having put ourselves through unnecessary physical upheaval. What we hear Paul saying in this letter is that only God can bring about the true change that affects us at our very core, by entering into our lives Himself and changing us from the inside out. He does that by healing our eyes and heart, giving us His perspective so as to attune us to a new way of living that gives life to others and honours creation.[48] This comes by way of revelation of His true character as He goes about being the triune God of grace in and among us.

---

[45] Simon Baker, *Ancient Rome: The Rise and Fall of an Empire* (BBC Books, 2007; EPub file), chapter III. This chapter on Nero shows the lengths that this Emperor goes to proclaim his impact on the Empire and his supremacy over it.

[46] Sometimes they tried driving out "evil" in each other through murder or by usurping the role and authority of one another in the Empire.

[47] Two books worth reading on the real meaning of "gospel" in the New Testament period are Scot McKnight, *The King Jesus Gospel: The Original Good News Revisited* (Grand Rapids, MI: Zondervan, 2011) and N.T. Wright, *How God Became King: The Forgotten Story of the Gospels* (New York: Harper One, 2012). However, note that Wright, much more than McKnight, is of the opinion that Paul's emphasis in relation to the gospel of King Jesus is a countercultural response to the so-called "gospel" that was being preached by the Roman emperors, who proclaimed themselves *soter* (Saviour) and King of the Empire. McKnight actually repudiates this notion – and in so doing ignores, I believe, a very crucial part of Paul's message here in Ephesians as well as in Romans and elsewhere.

[48] Paul describes in relational terms what some scholars explain him seeing in terms of substance. Either we see the recovered relationship effecting change in humanity, or we see Jesus "imputing righteousness". But if the latter, then what Paul describes as the Spirit's role has no intrinsic significance for our salvation.

A COMMUNITY THAT SPEAKS OF THE TRIUNE RELATIONSHIP

The Roman emperors professed to give life by taking it, but Jesus truly gives life by filling it. The concept of filling is not a pantheistic one in which the divine essence impersonally and molecularly fills every physical thing on earth; rather, it is a fullness of relationship that results when life is lived in honour of God's authority over all things and out of an awareness of His presence in His community. God's desire is for us to have the same relationship with Him and with each other that is enjoyed by the Persons of the Trinity, who "indwell" each other and live out their personhood by living in and out of each other. Paul's reference to "fullness" in this part of the letter is a reference to the triune character of living not just "with" each other but "in" each other.

In our North American Western culture, we are afraid to be that close to each other. Living in a culture permeated by the Enlightenment value of individualism, we can only dare to *hope* that someone else might want to be *with* us; never do we think or desire that we live *in* one another.[49] Yet "in" is what God desires. He wants to be "in" us.[50] He wants us to know the expansive love that comes from being in relationship with Him. The same love that the Father, Son, and Spirit have for each other is the love that God desires us to experience in relationship with Him and with one another.

This God that Paul is speaking of desires to be with His creation. He desires relationship with it. He longs for it to know His love and His character. As God's community, we live in the fullness of our relationship with the triune God of grace, who desires that all His creatures live in community with Him. God's community then becomes the entity in the world that demonstrates what it is to be fully human. To be fully human (as Paul will expound in chapter 2) is to be living in God's community where His fullness dwells, so that this fullness of relationship is expressed wherever the community lives. The community's expression of such a relationship with God is evidence of God filling the world as well. To continue with the theme of "indwelling", our living as the body of

---

[49] I find that we are fearful, in our Christian communities, of using the term "in" to refer to relationship, given that our culture has sexualized the idea into a physical act, and so we refrain from even speaking of it. But the language of "in", as used by Jesus on the night of the Last Supper (as recorded by John – specifically, in John 14:20, "…you will realize that I am in my Father, and you are in me, and I am in you." NIV), expresses a sense of "abiding", a relationship of sustained intimacy characterized by mutual acceptance, love, and embrace, with no malice, guile, or desire to take advantage. The result of "indwelling" in the Godhead is expressed in the voice of the Father over the Son at Jesus' baptism and transfiguration: "This is my Son in whom I am well pleased."
[50] Like the tent of meeting in the camp of Israel during the wandering in the wilderness. He wants to be in community with us.

Christ in community together is living "in" each other, expressing a quality of abiding and love that comes from being in relationship with God.

What Paul is talking about here is the expression of Jesus to the world through the community of believers, showing the world what God desires for the entire human race – that is, that He might dwell in all! If He has chosen the human race to be "holy and blameless in Christ", then surely His desire is for the human race to experience the fruit of that status. So God's community becomes an extension of Christ – the example of true humanity in whom the fullness of God is revealed. There will always be a distinction, since Christ will eternally be the one and only Lord over all things, but there is also an eternal connection between Christ and all who live in relationship with Him, expressing to the rest of the human race the same true humanity that he has.

Imagine what an incredible influence God's community can have in the world with such an understanding and relationship at its heart. Yet too often, church communities fall far short of what God has called us to be. We've become stale communities that mirror the surrounding economic, political, and cultural structures, existing at a distance from God rather than as communities who live out of the incredible inheritance of our adoption in Christ. We go about "rearranging the furniture" so to speak, rather than letting God's revelation go deep into the core of our being so that our understanding is redeemed and our perspective changed to view the world and others in relationship to the triune God of grace. Rather than accept each other as God's children, and so as brothers and sisters, we reject each other, insist on the differences between us, and take advantage of each other, all in the name of following Jesus.

It could be that we need to recognize, as N.T. Wright declares in his brief commentary on Paul's prison letters, that:

> …the power which raised Jesus from the dead and which will transform the whole world and flood it with His glory, is in fact available for us – And King Jesus has, as his hands and feet, his agents within the present world, the church. It is 'his body, the fullness of the one who fills all in all.' If only the church would realize this and act accordingly![51]

I think we often neglect to base our identity as Christians on the character of the philanthropic God who lavishes all His riches and blessings on us. We choose instead to hang on to our supposed identity as individuals who are responsible

---

[51] N. T. Wright, *Paul for Everyone: The Prison Letters: Ephesians, Philippians, Colossians* (Louisville, KY: Westminster John Knox Press, 2004) EPub File, p. 51.

for living a holy life in isolation, hoping that our own achieved obedience will be a satisfactory expression of our relationship with God. Rather than anchoring our trust and faith in the triune God of grace, we place it in the imagined God who demands restitution for our offence against His holiness. Paul nowhere mentions such a thing, nor paints such a portrait of God. Everything about the first chapter of this letter speaks of the triune God who, out of love, creates the human race and chooses to rescue it by the attachment of His Son to it as the one true human who comes to redeem humanity. Such good news is so desperately needed in the distorted and broken lives of our brothers and sisters who live unaware of it.

Paul's reference to resurrection echoes, in an expanded way, the Jewish anticipation of God putting all things right in the end. To recognize the power of God through the resurrection of Jesus in the present is to declare that the restoration of humanity is taking place now, and that God, by the same power, will continue to bring it to effect throughout the creation for its full and complete resurrection in the end. In the gospels, Jesus used the term "Kingdom of God" to refer to the fulfillment of God's plan now being revealed through Him in the present. The power that raised Christ is given to us as His community by the Spirit, so that living in that community we may reflect the transforming reality of resurrection to the world. By being "in Christ", God's community rules along with Christ, and through His community Christ exerts His authority over the powers of darkness.

All this is realized and enabled by the Spirit at work in the community that God the Father has created through adoption. In the latter half of the letter, Paul will go into more detail about this work of the Spirit.

Chapter Three

RESTORED TO OUR TRUE HUMANITY

Ephesians 2:1–7
You once lived like walking dead people – everything you did betrayed your humanity. You walked by the drum beat of this world and its lead drummer who fills the air with sounds of rebellion for his followers. We all at one time followed carnal desires, like so many others doing things that warranted the anger of a loving God.

But the God who loves us immensely and is so rich in mercy, even when we were living as walking dead people, made us alive in Christ (saving us by grace) and raised us up together with Him, seating us with Christ in God's realm. As His realm broke into our carnal existence, we were made alive to the riches of his unending grace through his kindness toward us in Christ Jesus.

TURNING DEAD PEOPLE INTO LIVING PEOPLE

Evil has dealt a death blow to humanity. People walk around in an empty existence, with the life given to them by God at creation all but drained out of them. They are mere shells of what they were created to be. Evil enslaves them to their base desires and causes them to do things that slowly destroy any remaining semblance of humanity. These people walk around like they are alive, but in reality they are dead inside. There is nothing alive about their humanity except a faint sense of what gave them life in the first place.

There is nothing sensational about this. It is a living hell, an existence where evil has us in its clutches and will not let go. And because of this we live in a state of being that is less than the humanity God intended at creation. Think of all the destructive abuses in our world that rip human beings apart and consign them to an animal-like existence, enslaved to carnal desires and without any moral compass; that is the picture, ultimately, of life lived to the drum beat of rebellion.

The world into which Jesus came and in which Paul wrote, the world of the Roman Empire in the first century AD, was rife with such abuses in a way that was particularly obvious. Human life was a commodity. With a large portion of the population classified as slaves, ownership of human life was characterized by a sense of entitlement and the legitimization of abuse.[52] Slaves were purchased from all over the Empire in a slave trade that would shock our present world.[53] Stripped naked in the market square,[54] they were eyed up and down and desired for all sorts of base intentions.[55] The culture of the Empire was so dehumanized by this that the Romans made a sport of publicly torturing marginalized and unwanted slaves in the local theatres of entertainment. It was as though the evil one was in charge.

Into this dark and sordid realm[56] God's love breaks through in the person of Christ. Humanity is rescued out of the clutches of evil and restored in Christ to the beauty in which it was fashioned at creation. Several times in this part of the letter, Paul uses the phrase "in Christ" to speak of how God the Son (the second person of the Trinity) entered this dark human existence to save it from the destructive path it was on. We were made alive again in the emergence of a realm where God is on the throne and Christ is seated at His side, holding a place for true humanity to be in relationship with the triune God of grace.

When Christ was raised from the dead, we were all raised with Him, solidifying God's attachment to humanity. Released from walking death row, we now walk in newness of life; no longer slaves to sin, we are subjects of a loving King who has given us the richness of his love, grace, and mercy. As in so many stories told in film today, our true identity rises out of the ashes of a

---

[52] See Jennifer A. Glancy, *Slavery in Early Christianity* (Minneapolis: Fortress Press, 2006), p. 51, where she describes the bodily abuse suffered by slaves in the Empire.

[53] See Richard Bauckham, *Jesus: A Very Short Introduction* (Oxford: Oxford University Press, 2011), p. 20. "The benefits of peace and prosperity that Rome claimed to give its subjects could not obscure the fact that the empire served primarily the prosperity of the Romans and the local elites who supported them."

[54] See K. R. Bradley, *Slaves and Masters in the Roman Empire: A Study in Social Control* (New York: Oxford University Press, 1987), p. 115, where he states, "Among other indignities slaves on the block might find themselves …having to appear naked, having their feet whitened with chalk to show their foreign origin, or being obliged to carry placards advertising their own qualities."

[55] See James S. Jeffers, *The Greco-Roman World of the New Testament Era: Exploring the Background of Early Christianity* (Downers Grove, IL: Intervarsity Press, 1999), p. 223.

[56] F. F. Bruce, *The Epistles to the Colossians, to Philemon and to the Ephesians: The New International Commentary on the New Testament* (Grand Rapids, MI: Eerdmans, 1984), p. 282. "The 'domain of the air' in fact, is another way of indicating the 'heavenly realm' which, according to Eph. 6:12, is the abode of those principalities and powers, 'world rulers of this darkness' and 'spiritual forces of wickedness' against which the people of Christ wage war." Cf. Fee, *God's Empowering Presence*, p. 680: "The false 'spirit's' realm is also in the heavenlies; but God by his power raised Christ to sit above the powers and to be head over them for the church (1:20–23). From here Paul will go on to emphasize that God has also raised his people to sit 'in the heavenlies' with Christ, and therefore they are no longer under the dominion of, or in fear of, the 'spirit who is now at work among the disobedient.'"

false existence, but the difference in the story told by Paul is that a Redeemer has literally entered our human existence to deal a death blow to sin and cancel its ravaging of the human race.[57] The point is not whether we deserved such an existence or whether we lacked the moral resolve to free ourselves (although that is a related issue); the point is that evil has been successful in undermining creation, but will not triumph because God will not allow it to do so. The Old Testament narrative reveals God's promise to redeem creation, which He does through Jesus – with whom, according to this passage, we are raised up and seated in God's "realm". God's realm stands in contrast to this world, in which the lead drummer – Satan – drums to the beat of rebellious existence. A battle is being waged by the true realm against the false one, so that the death march of Satan will no longer lead humanity astray. The true Ruler of the heavenly realms will rescue humanity from the false ruler and restore it to life.

Robert Suh, in an article entitled "The Use of Ezekiel 37 in Ephesians 2", points out the uncanny similarity between the two passages, suggesting that Paul used the structure and content of Ezekiel 37 to craft this part of his letter.[58] In the Ezekiel passage, the prophet is given a vision by God of a valley containing the dead bones of the nation of Israel, and God shows the prophet that this nation will be brought to life again through the power of His desire for their redemption and resurrection. It is likely that Paul, here in Ephesians 2, is expanding Ezekiel's national vision into a cosmic one in which God is at work through Christ to enliven the whole human race.

Paul shows the determination of this lavish, gift-giving, creating, redeeming God to embark on a plan of rescue for the human race in which we are brought to life again through Jesus, no longer slaves to evil but alive as God's creation.[59] Unlike the gods of pagan myth who devour humanity, this God lives to restore life to his creation. I am referring inclusively to "creation" here because all of nature is subject to its connection to humanity, and suffers under humanity's enslavement in its "walking dead" state; Paul lays this out clearly in Romans

---

[57] In most stories in the theatre, the main character finds the resolve from within to be released from present evil or enlightened to a different sort of life.

[58] Robert Suh, "The Use of Ezekiel 37 in Ephesians 2," *Journal of the Evangelical Theological Society* (December 2007), pp. 715–733. Suh discusses this as an example of the intertextuality evidenced in the New Testament, whereby New Testament writers based some of their writing on thematic and linguistic constructions of passages in the Old Testament. Even if one does not agree with all that Suh proposes in terms of the comparison, one cannot deny that there is some parallelism between these two passages.

[59] Ibid, page 725. Suh acknowledges that "[t]he focus of both passages [Ezekiel 37 and Ephesians 2] is not the dead status of sinful people, but rather the divine work of granting new life to his people, that is, God's decisive action of recreation of his people."

8:15ff.[60] God never meant for humanity to live in such emptiness and alienation from the rest of creation.

Ephesians 2:8–10

For we have been saved by grace through [the] faith [of Jesus].[61] It is God's gift to us, not based on our own doing, so that no one can boast. We are his masterpiece, created in Christ Jesus to do good works in keeping with how God intended for us to live.

RESTORED TO TRUE LIVING

The grace of God has accomplished our salvation from a life destined for death. We were not truly living; we were dead inside. We were living a life that God never intended for us to live, for a life lived apart from God is a life that is less than fully human. But because of His lavish blessing, God gives us the gift of life lived in true humanity. This humanity is not a zombie-like existence, but a living out our lives as His masterpieces, according to the design and intent He had from the beginning. We were created with the care and artistry of a cosmic Sculptor who crafted human beings to live in harmony with Himself and with creation.

Rather than living out the works of death that characterize our former zombie-like existence, destroying ourselves and others, we have received at God's hands the gift of living a life of goodness that, in turn, brings life to the rest of creation[62]. Humanity is intended to mirror to the creation the goodness of what it means to be in relationship with Father, Son, and Spirit. The same creative energy of love that flows out of the Trinity, bringing good to our world, is the loving energy God has recovered for us, so that we bring good to others and to the rest of creation because we live in communion with Him.

---

[60] Paul mentions the creation being subjected to futility and enduring labour pains while awaiting the full redemption of humanity.

[61] The phrase "of Jesus" is my addition, but it is consistent with the context and with Paul's implication. We must not allow ourselves to be confused by the phrase "through faith", interpreting it as an act on our part that precedes and ensures the receiving of the gift of salvation that God has given. The context clearly shows that there is no room to boast about any action on the part of "dead humanity" to regain a state of true humanity; it is a gift that God has acquired for us. This is the implication of vs. 5 as well – in fact, of Paul's whole emphasis so far on the reality brought about "in Christ" – and it will be confirmed by the later part of chapter 2. I can live with our resting in the fact that God accomplishes this for us without any satisfaction of conditions on our part.

[62] Paul uses the Greek word *"peripateo"* (περιπατησωμεν), literally "the way we should walk", to speak of the way humanity is truly meant to live. It is usually translated "live", but "walk" captures the intentionality, activity, and concreteness of what is conveyed in terms of our purposefully moving along a path laid out for us by God, carrying out the actions that befit our true humanity.

This outcome of "good works" has a cosmic significance. It is not only that God has saved us in Christ so that we now can do good works as the fruit and expression of our connection and relationship with God,[63] but also that these works we do as His community are a participation in God's plan to purge the whole world of evil and restore all of creation to its proper existence, and so they have a cosmic impact, a ripple effect that flows outward from that community. Paul points out that God "intended for us to live" this way, echoing the idea in chapter 1 of God having "marked out beforehand" His plan of rescue for humanity. Paul also uses this idea of "preparing ahead of time" in Romans 9:23, where he is building an argument concerning God's plan to unite Jews and Gentiles together into one community.[64] Here in Ephesians, we will see the same theme of unity expressed in the very next part of the letter! The point is that these good works of ours are part of a bigger redemptive picture with a significance beyond our own immediate lives.

In other words, our "good works" consist not merely in decent personal behaviour that is in keeping with the character of our relationship with Christ. It is more than that. We are now collectively God's community, "the body of Christ in and for the world",[65] and this new community that is God's masterpiece will have a redeeming, restorative effect on the world, exposing the darkness of evil and revealing the light of Christ and His new humanity.[66] It will do God's will in offering His healing to the people and other creatures that it will encounter, and will treat broken humanity and suffering creation not according to their corrupt, evil existence, but as God sees them through Christ. As Paul describes so eloquently at the end of Galatians, this community is to see humanity and

---

[63] As D. Edmond Hiebert makes clear in his article "God's Creative Masterpiece," *Direction* 23:1 (Spring, 1994), p. 119, "We work not to be saved, but because we have been saved. Good works are the fruit, never the root, of salvation."

[64] Ibid, p. 121. "The aorist tense verb rendered 'afore prepared' (*proetoimasen*) is a compound form which occurs elsewhere in the New Testament only in Romans 9:23. The simple verb means 'to prepare, to make ready,' while the preposition *pro*, 'before, beforehand,' stresses God's action in preparing these good works for believers has already taken place; the aorist tense views that work as accomplished. The preparation of those works took place in time past and now awaits to be performed by believers as they appear on the scene of history."

[65] N. T. Wright, *Justification*, p. 171. "Yes, 'good works' will undoubtedly include 'moral behaviour.' But Paul is more interested, as he is in Philippians 1:27–39 and Philippians 4:8–9, about the public face of the church in the world, about Christians shining in the world as lights in a dark place (Ephesians 4:17–5:20; compare Philippians 2:12–18). This will involve Christians behaving according to radically different standards than the world's, but the point of this is not simply 'because you now need to be virtuous' but 'because the church is the body of Christ in and for the world.'"

[66] See Chapter 7 of this commentary, "Living as Children of Light".

the world through the redemptive work of the cross, and so in its status of new creation.[67] God's community will be the humanity that He desired from the beginning, living in harmony with Himself, with one another, and with the rest of creation so that all God has made may live at its fullest capacity.[68] True humanity lived out in the world will restore order in the creation and peace among the nations.

In the latter half of chapter 2, Paul will emphasize how proximity to God is key to what Christ has done within the human condition, restoring harmonious relationship to the human race in a way that brings peace. "Peace" in the Roman Empire came at the cost of bloodshed and violence, with crosses to remind the people how any sign of hostility toward the Empire would promptly be squashed.[69] By contrast, Paul will show that God brings about peace for the human race through the elimination of hostility in the person of Christ himself. It is not God's way to take life in order to ensure peace by coercion, but to give life in order to establish peace by new creation. This giving of life will now take the form of God gathering all humanity, Jew and Gentile, into Christ, reconciling and ordering everything on earth and in the heavenly realms under King Jesus according to His plan.

---

[67] See Galatians 6:14ff, where Paul writes, "But to me may it not be to boast except in the cross of our Lord Jesus Christ, through whom to me the world has been crucified and I to the world. For neither circumcision is anything nor uncircumcision, but a new creation. And as many as will keep in line with this rule, peace upon them and mercy, even to the Israel of God." This is not an encouragement to ignore or avoid the world, but to see it through the lens of the crucified One – as the world for which Christ died, and so as the new creation that He has made. It is very telling that Paul follows the statement with a blessing of peace upon those who continue in this way! Paul will speak of this same peace in the next passage here in Ephesians.

[68] Echoes resound of God's mandate to Adam and Eve in Genesis, to "be fruitful and multiply and bring order".

[69] Richard Horsley, *Paul and Empire*, p. 18. "Augustus was the prince of peace in foreign affairs, but it was **pax** in the Roman sense; **making a pact after conquest**."

Chapter Four

TAKING AWAY HOSTILITY AND SEPARATION

Ephesians 2:11–13

Remember how you were as Gentiles, living in the flesh, called outsiders by those who considered themselves insiders according to their own works. At that time you were living apart from Christ, alienated from the nation of Israel and strangers to the promises of God, without hope and godless in the world. Now in Christ Jesus, you who were far away have been brought near by the blood of Christ.

WE HAVE BEEN BROUGHT NEAR

There is irony in Paul's description of the Gentiles. According to Roman imperial propaganda, it was every nation's privilege to have been brought into the Empire so as to enjoy its benefits, even if it was through the blood of their fellow countrymen slain at the hands of the Romans themselves. But here, Paul describes how the shedding of the blood of Christ, God's own Son, has brought them near to the God who lavishes His great gifts on His creation. Whether intentionally or unintentionally, Paul's words critique the story being told in the Empire. The emperor gathers the aliens into the Empire by the sword, shedding the blood of enemies and native conscripts alike,[70] but God gathers the alien into relationship with Himself through the blood of His own Son.

The Gentiles were labelled by those who claimed to know God and his law, specifically the Jews, as outsiders[71] and not part of the covenant people God had called out as His own. This meant they were excluded from the great promises of God that Paul refers to as the mystery of God's plan. Clearly, though, Israel herself

---

[70] See Jeffers, p. 221, where he states that "...three circumstances helped transform Rome into a 'slave society': the great increase in the landholdings of rich Romans, the depletion of the native workforce as its members were conscripted to fight its continual wars, *and the introduction of massive numbers of captured enemies into the slave market*" [italics mine].

[71] I chose to interpret "uncircumcised" as the word picture that represents Gentiles as being outside the covenant relationship that Jews believed they had with God by virtue of their ethnic identity. Paul makes it clear that it was the Jews (who saw themselves as ethnically connected to God), and not God, who identified Gentiles as outsiders.

had misheard the promises, since their goal was not to alienate the Gentiles but to gather all nations to the Father.[72]

What is clear in this letter about the shedding of Jesus' blood is that it ended the Gentiles' estrangement from the mystery of God's plan to gather all humanity to Himself, and so created one new humanity out of the two. The shedding of blood is part of the imagery of sacrifice, of course, but the controlling concept invoked by Paul to make sense of this sacrifice is adoption. This sacrifice by Jesus breaks the estrangement and distance between God and humanity — not only the Jewish people to whom the promises were originally entrusted (who thought they were already near to God despite their rebellion), but also the Gentiles for whose equal benefit the promises were made. It brings *all* humanity close to God, and re-establishes a true humanity — remembering, in chapter 1, Paul's use of the word "cancel" to denote the act of Christ in His sacrifice breaking the cycle of perpetual sin that alienates us from God. His sacrifice (climaxing in His death but integrally taking in his life, death, resurrection, and ascension) stops the decay of the human race and forever breaks the bondage in which it is held by sin.

Underlying this is the notion of revelation that Paul spoke about in the latter part of chapter 1. A revelation has now been made to the Gentiles that was hidden[73] in God's words to Israel. This revelation is that the God of the Jews desired that the Gentiles also share in the same covenant promise. In the following verses Paul will point out that *both* groups are reconciled by the act of Jesus, who brings them together through His sacrifice. Relational proximity to God is realized by God's work in Christ, and not by the assumptions and presumptions of those who declare their own proximity to God. Jews who declared their proximity to God at the expense of the Gentiles' distance were re-interpreting God's connection to humanity in exclusive terms that did not reflect God's heart. Paul understands that God set Israel apart *for* the world, not *from* the world.

This has implications for us believers today. In the same way, we need to be careful how we who profess to be close to God define ourselves in relation to others. If we define ourselves as close to God in contrast to those who are "far" or "distant", then we are playing on an alienation that God does not desire or intend. We need to be careful that the same exclusivism that the Jews practised

---

[72] The gathering of the Gentiles is an obvious theme in the Major Prophets, especially Isaiah.

[73] Its status as "hidden" is due more to Israel's inadequate understanding of and witness to God's plan than to God's deliberate concealment of it; the intention to include the nations in the covenant blessing is communicated to Israel throughout the Old Testament.

and celebrated does not become our own prejudice as well. The intent of this part of Paul's letter is quite clear: God's goal, accomplished in Jesus, is that all humanity[74] is transformed and gathered into one people. And now that it has been accomplished, we are called to witness to this fact in the world, just as the Jews were called to witness to God's plan among the nations in preparation for His redemptive work.

The challenge to us as we read Paul has to do with the language we choose for those who have yet to know this great mystery of God's plan for humanity. We tend to call them "lost", evoking a picture of their wandering aimlessly through life without any connection to God. This is not the way Paul sees it. In fact, in his address to the Stoics and Epicureans in Athens, recorded by Luke in the book of Acts, Paul points out that "God is not far from anyone", that all of us "live and move and exist in Him" and "are His children".[75] In fact, he states that anyone can find Him, and this ability to "find" God is based on His having made humanity from one person in the first place.[76] The fact that the Athenians had found Him already was evidenced in their erecting a statue to the "unknown God"; what kept them from enjoying fellowship with this God, from worshipping Him in a way that was in keeping with His character, was "ignorance". In Ephesians we see that this ignorance came through division and hostility that was fuelled by evil, causing humanity to turn in on itself rather than exist as God's cosmic family. The solution to restoring humanity to one cosmic family would come through another Man who would bring unity by driving out division and hostility.[77]

---

[74] The mention of "Jews and Gentiles" is code for "everyone", that is, all categories of people. This is made clear by Paul in chapter 2.

75 Acts 17:26ff.

[76] The biblical creation story, as alluded to by Paul in the discourse in Acts 17, points to God's desire to reach all people based on His design of linking men and women together. Evil undermines such community and harmony over the course of history, but God does not give up His desire; His goal is to recover harmony and community for humanity by destroying evil.

[77] This understanding of Paul's is the essential result of his encounter with Jesus, which made clear to him that God did not entertain a preference of one people group over another. Through Jesus' question, "Why are you persecuting me?", it dawns on Paul that God is connected to everyone, and as such is in the process of rescuing everyone.

Ephesians 2:14–22

Jesus is our peace, making us one by tearing down the dividing wall of hostility. He did this in his flesh, rendering powerless[78] the law with its commands and decrees by taking Jews and Gentiles and making them, in himself, one new humanity and so restoring peace. He did this so that he might reconcile both Jews and Gentiles into one body by putting to death hostility and division through his work on the cross. Having done this, he then announced the good news of peace to those who were far away and to those who are near. Now through Jesus we both have access by one Spirit to the Father. You are no longer strangers and foreigners belonging nowhere, but citizens of God's community built on the foundation of the Apostles and Prophets; its cornerstone is Jesus Christ himself, in whom the whole community is joined together, growing into God's holy dwelling place. You are being built into this community where God dwells by His Spirit.

CREATING ONE NEW HUMANITY

There is no avoiding the impression that what Paul says in this passage is countercultural and obliquely critical of the Empire. The emperor declares his fatherhood over all people and gives his pledge of peace, yet the culture of the Empire is characterized by prejudice, civil unrest, violence, and dehumanization. In contrast, Paul declares in this passage that true peace is established by Jesus, who builds us into God's community. What ailed the human heart in the Empire was alienation; in Paul's day, citizenship was difficult to obtain, and usually depended on bribery of the state officials, so that whole classes of people were excluded from the community and denied the privilege of citizenship.[79] In the

---

[78] I have chosen to translate καταργηω as "rendering powerless". In his *New International Dictionary of New Testament Theology*, vol. 1 (Grand Rapids, IL: Zondervan, 1975), Colin Brown indicates that the content of this participle is "God's putting out of action…destructive powers which threaten man's spiritual well-being" (p. 73). This meaning is based on Paul's identification of the Law as having been taken advantage of by sin and so made death to man as outlined in Romans 7. In this passage in Ephesians, part of that "death" is the hostility that the Law created between Jew and Gentile. This is confirmed by Bauer as well, who points out that "the Law is made invalid" (Walter Bauer, ed., *A Greek-English Lexicon of the New Testament and Other Early Christian Literature*, 2nd Edition; University of Chicago Press, 1979, p. 417).

[79] There were varying degrees of openness to citizenship by the Roman elite. For the most part, they felt it their commission from the gods to protect the integrity of the Empire by being particular as to who received citizenship. Early in the Empire's history, the Senate proved influential in determining who received citizenship. Later on, during the period of the emperors, some of them would offer citizenship to the masses to appease popular displeasure over the emperor's leadership. It was also used as a political move to gain favour. See Simon Baker, *Ancient Rome: The Rise and Fall of an Empire* (BBC Books, 2007; EPub file), p. xx.

community being built by Christ, on the other hand, everyone belongs, and the alien is welcomed into proximity to God who created the human race.

Broken humanity, divided across civil and religious lines, is in a state of alienation and hostility. In fact, even those whom Paul describes as being "near" have misunderstood the nature of God's community and are at cross-purposes with His plan to bring peace and harmony to His creation. Commissioned as God's people to gather all nations to Him, they did the opposite and created distance through their sense of exclusive identity and relationship to God.[80] Not only was the world broken, but those who had been called to be vessels of God's healing and blessing had refused to do so. There was a need for radical intervention, for someone to enter into the human condition and recover it for God's purposes.

Paul declares that what Jesus has accomplished on the cross is the elimination of division and hostility created by the Law, which set Jews and Gentiles at odds with each other. We can add to our understanding of this by drawing on Paul's comments elsewhere regarding the effect of the Law on the human race. Both in Galatians and Romans, Paul points out that the purpose of the Law was not to save but to condemn;[81] the condemnation comes as sin takes advantage of the Law and makes it death to us.[82] But this rendering of condemnation on all people then allows God to show his mercy on all.[83] In other words, by taking advantage

---

[80] For the sake of brevity I have not mentioned the fact, clear in the Old Testament, that Israel desired God's presence to be restored to their land and community. Although alienating the Gentile, Israel still longed for God's presence among them again; this is shown by their zeal for the temple in Jerusalem, which was the dwelling place of God. But God was doing a new thing now; the idea of the temple as His holy dwelling among the Jews would be turned inside out. According to N. T. Wright, "…Paul is declaring that the living God is constructing a new Temple. It consists, not of stones, arches, pillars and altars, but of human beings. Some Jews had already explored the idea that community, rather than a building, might be the place where God would really and truly take up his residence." In *Paul for Everyone: The Prison Letters* (Louisville, KY: Westminster John Knox Press, 2004) EPub File, p. 95.

[81] Galatians 3:19, "The law was added for the sake of transgressions." What exactly is meant by "for the sake of" here is not immediately obvious. The NLT translates this (somewhat poorly, in my view) as "It was given to show people how guilty they are", while The Message reads, "The purpose of the law was to keep a sinful people in the way of salvation …". I believe Peterson succeeds better at maintaining the intent of Paul's discussion in Galatians 3.

[82] Romans 7:7–13. In this passage Paul speaks of sin taking advantage of the Law, which is good, and making it evil, condemning humanity in their fallen state and offering no way out.

[83] Romans 11:32, "For God has imprisoned all people in their own disobedience so he could have mercy on everyone" (NLT). This is the controlling verse in Romans, giving clarity to Paul's message to the Jews and Gentiles in the Roman churches. Paul explains that there is no ground for boasting in our respective ethnic identities, as there is no advantage either way when it comes to relationship with God. It is all based on Christ bringing us to the Father.

of God's Law and perpetuating hostility in the human race, evil has only created an ideal scenario for God's mercy, whereby God through Christ puts to death the effect of the Law and creates a new humanity, free of the power of sin and grounded in the person of Christ.

The fact was that Israel took the Law (Torah) to be a badge or symbol of their belonging to God. Paul's argument is that because they were unable to keep the Law, what they viewed as a badge actually worked toward their own condemnation: like the Gentiles, they too were plunged into sin by evil and needed rescuing. This is the reality that Paul outlines in chapters 2 and 3 of Romans. Both Jews and Gentiles needed restoration of their broken relationship with God.[84] The way God would do this was by sending His Son, the one true Israelite who was faithful to God's covenant to rescue the human race through the specially prepared nation of Israel.[85] God's plan from the beginning was to bring all nations together, as evidenced in His promise to Abraham. Although Paul does not mention Abraham in Ephesians, he does so in other letters, and references the significance of God's covenant with him as a key piece in God's plan to gather humanity into one family in relationship with Himself.[86] All this lies in the background here in Ephesians as Paul describes what Christ (Israel's Messiah) has done in bringing the two people groups together.

The mention of "citizenship" raises the content of this passage from the level of a personal transformation to that of a communal transformation. It is no less than the very fabric of the human race that God has affected through Jesus. That is, the essence of the change God has brought about is that we now *belong* and therefore together constitute a community. Paul describes a change in status from *strangers and foreigners belonging nowhere* to *citizens of God's community where He dwells*. One needs to read only once through the Old Testament to appreciate

---

[84] Gordon Fee, *God's Empowering Presence*, p. 685. "Equally sinful, both have been equally given life and have been raised together and seated together in the heavenlies in Christ. Thus we have another of the 'Spirit's blessings': not only reconciliation with one another through Christ, but reconciliation with God through Christ; and our being together in the one Spirit in God's very presence attests that God has brought it off."

[85] N. T. Wright, *Justification*, p.203. "What was lacking, as we saw in Romans 2:21–24 and particularly, and sharply, in Romans 3:3, was faithfulness on the part of Israel, not some kind of meritorious behaviour through which Israel would rescue itself, but a faithfulness to God and his covenant purposes that would enable Israel to live up to its calling as the light to the dark world and so on (Romans 2:17–20)."

[86] See Galatians 3:15–29 and Romans 4. N. T. Wright also points out the narrative in Deuteronomy 27–30 as connected to the Abrahamic covenant, where God pronounces both blessings and curses on Israel and a promise of restoration as His people following a period of exile. See N. T. Wright, *Justification*, pp. 63–67.

that God has been about the business of restoring His presence and relationship with the human race since the Fall. The appearance of Jesus brings this plan to fruition, and so Paul orients his readers to that reality over against competing views embraced by the culture of the day. What is outstanding about the result of Christ's restorative work is not that "individual Jews and Gentiles alike now have access to the Father – but that both of them as one new humanity have such access."[87] In a real sense, this new humanity is a community that transcends ethnic and national boundaries. Jews and Gentiles stand hand in hand in joint relationship to God because of Christ and by His Spirit.

Through the work of Christ, Jews and Gentiles now have *access by one Spirit to the Father*. This statement by Paul contains echoes of the words of the Major Prophets to Israel. God's promise was to put His Spirit into His people so that they might keep His commands and be in fellowship with Him.[88] Giving them, by the work of Christ, a heart that has the capacity to receive what God has to give in terms of His connection with humanity, God restores the human race to Himself. God laid the foundation for all of this long ago and has built on it continually ever since. Jesus is the very centre of this foundation; He is the pivotal point on which it all hinges and endures. It is no longer through the temple in Jerusalem that humanity gains access to God;[89] it is now God's community, where His Spirit is present and Jews and Gentiles dwell together in Christ, that is the place of access to God. There is and will be no ruler on earth that can accomplish this; although many have tried, no one has been capable of doing so. Jesus is the one true King through whom God's new community will rise, reaching out to the human race so as to bring peace to every human heart.[90]

---

[87] Gordon Fee, *God's Empowering Presence*, p. 683: "Jew and Gentile stand together as one people in God's presence, with old distinctions no longer having significance."

[88] Ezekiel 36:26; Jeremiah 24:7.

[89] N. T. Wright, *Justification*, p. 172. "The image of the dividing wall is, pretty certainly, taken from the Jerusalem temple, with its sign warning Gentiles to come no further. That has gone in Christ, because in him a new temple is constructed." Cf. Fee, *God's Empowering Presence*, p. 683: "... 'in the one Spirit' replaces temple as the place of 'access' into the presence of God."

[90] In his book *How God Became King*, N. T. Wright unfolds how Jesus fulfills Israel's expectation of God ruling over the land once again. Based on what the prophets wrote, Jews expected that God's story would culminate in His reigning over them once again and delivering them from their oppressors. This is the same kind of language that the gospel writers use in relation to Jesus' ministry on earth; it is in the context of Israel's story that the Jesus story makes sense. Wright points out in the chapter on "The Story of Israel" (page 282) that the Jewish leaders rejected the return of God to rule over them, and instead pledged their allegiance to Caesar. It is this that the gospel writers show Jesus critiquing and challenging in his own identity and mission. Paul advances the same view here in Ephesians chapter 2.

This is an incredible message, written in a time and place in which many political leaders and philosophers continually promised such peace for humanity, but never delivered. They also promised a connection to God, but it never transpired.[91] There are those whom Paul will describe later in chapter 5 as being "asleep"[92] and not cognizant of what God has done for them through Jesus. Paul will encourage his readers to take up their place in God's new community and live out their new humanity so that others might come to know God as the wonderful Father who brings peace.

The Trinitarian focus is obvious. In this new community, Father, Son, and Spirit are directly involved, present and indwelling the community, directing it toward its inheritance as described by Paul in chapter 1. There will be no other community that offers the human race the kind of relationship that God's holy community does, where He dwells by His Spirit, sharing the love He has for His Son with us. This is exactly where God wants us, and exactly where we find our true identity and purpose as human beings. In the 1st century AD, under Roman rule, such a community represented a humanizing alternative amid routine and ruthless dehumanization.[93]

---

[91] See Martin Goodman, *The Roman World: 44 BC – 180 AD* (London, UK: Routledge, 2002), p. 299, where he points out that emperor worship did not begin until the imperial period. The emperor cult begun by Augustus Caesar promised that a direct connection to the gods existed in the person of the Emperor, but such a distinction never truly made a difference for the common person in the Empire except to offer another object of religious devotion among many to choose from.

[92] Ephesians 5:14.

[93] See Rodney Stark, *The Rise of Christianity* (San Francisco: Harper Collins, 1996), specifically chapter 9, "Opportunity and Organization". Stark draws attention to the huge impact of the early Christian community on the people of the Empire through their acts of benevolence and their general care for their neighbour. Stark points out that "…what Christianity gave to its converts was nothing less than their humanity."

Chapter Five

FROM MYSTERY TO KNOWLEDGE

Ephesians 3:1–9

It is for all this that I, Paul, am a prisoner of Christ Jesus for you outsiders; you may have heard how I was commissioned to share the grace of God given to me for you as it came to me in a revelation, where God made known to me the mystery of His plan as I just briefly laid out. By reading this you are able to have insight into the mystery of Christ, which generations past did not know about but which has now been revealed to His holy apostles and the prophets by the Spirit.[94] *By this I mean how the Gentiles have full privileges in God's community and can share in [God's promise] in Christ through the Good News. I became a servant of this Good News by the gift of God's grace, because of God's power at work in me. Imagine, this grace was given to me, less than the least of all the holy ones, to share with you outsiders the unsearchable riches of Christ and to open up the mystery hidden throughout history in the God who created all things!*

EXCEEDS ALL EXPECTATIONS

At times we might look at something we have written and be surprised at what we read. Looking at the finished product, we wonder how we ever could have written it. We think, "How could that have come out of me, when I walk around on a daily basis saying things that don't sound right and contradict the laws of language?"[95] What Paul expresses in this first half of chapter 3 is not that peculiar in terms of language use, but it is downright spectacular in terms of content. Being a Jew with Hebrew thoughts in one's heart does not always jive well with expressing oneself in the Greek language, but when Paul examines what he wrote in chapters 1 and 2, he begins chapter 3 with a sense of awe and wonder. What he has written about the mystery of God's plan is none other than the very heart of God for His creation from before the beginning of time. Having realized that God has used him to reveal

---

[94] I'm most certain that Paul is here referencing the teaching of Jesus to the twelve disciples — now apostles — as well as the writings of the Prophets in the Old Testament who spoke of this mystery.

[95] My first language was not English, so at times I can say things in the English language that sound very peculiar and cause listeners to say, "What in the world are you saying?"

this, he stumbles on a very sacred moment that causes him to pause and soak in the wonder for a bit longer!

Paul recalls to his readers how he was miraculously converted on the road to Damascus and given the call to bring the Good News of God's plan to the Gentiles. It was all a mystery until God revealed it to him through Jesus' appearance. Paul, who was then Saul of Tarsus, a devout Jew who could boast of faultlessly following God's law,[96] had been unaware of the "immense and infinite wisdom of God" (vs. 10) in planning to create one humanity in the person of His Son, Jesus Christ. He could not have imagined that this act on God's part would remove all hostility and separation in the human race and create an unprecedented peace and harmony of men and women in fellowship with each other and with God. And now he is the bearer of this news to the Gentiles!

There is a sense of cosmic timing in all of this. Paul remarks that this mystery was not known before. No one seemed to grasp what God was doing until Jesus appeared on the scene and revealed God's heart to the apostles. This revelation, in turn, shed light on what the prophets of old had spoken about: how God would draw all nations to Himself and restore the earth to the splendour He intended it to have from the beginning. Echoes of Isaiah resound loudly in Paul's words in chapters 1 and 2, about harmony and peace wiping out hatred and violence.[97] And there are echoes of Ezekiel's prophecy about the cleansing that God would bring by His Spirit to the human heart, so that men and women would be able to be faithful and obedient, living in unhindered relationship with Him.[98]

In God's community, defined by the person and work of Christ and the cooperation and involvement of the Spirit, there are no more outsiders. Everyone belongs. Jews and Gentiles are brought into harmonious fellowship with each other that rivals all other fellowships.[99] Like one of the lowly hobbits in J. R. R. Tolkien's *The Lord of the Rings,* Paul looks upon himself as the least of all human beings on the earth, less than all others in God's community. How could God give him such a commission as sharing this great news of His secret plan, and with such unlikely people? And yet there is something about God choosing Paul for such a task that speaks of how He goes about fulfilling this great mystery. Surely there were other candidates more equipped and more in tune with God's heart than Paul was. There must have been "holier" saints that were worthier of

---

[96] Philippians 3:6.

[97] See Isaiah 11:10ff; Isaiah 56:3ff.

[98] See Ezekiel 36:25–27.

[99] Yes, even that great Fellowship of the Ring!

such a calling, rather than this one who had persecuted those to whom God had already begun revealing the mystery. Yet, *because* he had been the persecutor of his own countrymen and the faithful followers of Christ, there was no one who better understood the depth of God's grace revealed in Jesus than Saul of Tarsus. The ideal candidate to speak credibly to others of the blessing and riches of God's grace was someone who had been forgiven much.

Paul calls himself a prisoner and a servant. Both terms evoke the base character of those who were despised in the Roman Empire. A life of servitude was looked down upon by Roman freemen and freewomen, but there is no greater title or role in the context of God's Kingdom than those who bring the Good News of peace into the brokenness of human existence.[100] For Paul, this was something he did both as a servant to the Gentiles and as a prisoner in Caesar's own backyard, sharing the Good News of God's grace.[101] This is the Good News whose power causes dead people to live again! People subject to the vilest existence filled with subjugation and abuse, enslaved by evil to their base desires to walk the earth as less than fully human, are made whole again when their eyes are opened to the revelation of God's love in Jesus Christ. God's power was at work in the words and actions of Paul the apostle, through whom the recounting of God's secret plan was accompanied by signs and God's mighty deeds: healings, deliverance, and people exchanging confusion for clarity, abuse for embrace, brokenness for wholeness, alienation for acceptance.

This Good News told a different story from the imperial one, reminding the marginalized of the Empire that what defined them was not the culture of the Empire but the very God of grace who was their Creator and Redeemer. This God had created them for greater things! He had designed them to be masterpieces of His creation, enhancing the world around them. This was Good News for those who lived in squalor in the tenements of the Empire's overcrowded cities. Gentiles heard the Good News and their eyes were opened to a different life that ennobled the regular course of street dwellers in the Great Empire.[102] The Imperial Cult boasted of the presence of God among the

---

[100] Paul will later quote the passage in Isaiah about the "beautiful feet" of those who bring the "Good News of peace" when he calls on God's community to battle alongside Him against evil. See Chapter Nine of this book, "Battling Evil".

[101] Acts 28:15–30.

[102] Rodney Stark, in *The Rise of Christianity*, pp. 150–156, outlines the misery of life in Rome. The poor were housed in crowded, unsanitary buildings, with the threat of disease or asphyxiation from lack of proper ventilation for cooking fires, and their buildings often collapsed. Streets were filled with the garbage of everyday human consumption, resulting in a lingering stench and the continual breeding of all kinds of disease.

people,[103] but the conditions of the Empire betrayed this claim; the Good News shared by Paul, on the other hand, was evidenced by a community that lived inclusively, welcoming all who desired to be part of it. In this community were love, peace, and harmony; people were "patient"[104] with each other, knowing that all were on a journey of recovery and restoration. The privilege of belonging was to know the mind and heart of God, who loved His creation! And this true knowledge of God and humanity, acquired by encounter with the living Lord, was the impetus for acts of social kindness. The overwhelming behaviour of the Christian community toward others attracted people from all walks of life who wanted to become part of such a loving and caring fellowship.[105] This was the community whose God – 250 years later – would be acknowledged by the emperor himself to be Lord and King of heaven and earth![106]

Ephesians 3:10–13[107]

Through God's community, the immense and infinite[108] wisdom of God is made known to the highest rulers and authorities. God planned it this way so that it is accomplished in Christ Jesus our Lord, in whom we have assured access in the confidence of His faith. So don't lose heart over my suffering for you which makes you famous as His community.

SURPASSING ALL EARTHLY POWERS

It is quite amazing to think of how this small community of believers, made up of Jews and Gentiles, could cause such a ripple throughout the Empire. Here were

---

[103] See Richard Gordon, "The Veil of Power", in *Paul and Empire: Religion and Power in Roman Imperial Society*, ed. Richard A. Horsley (Harrisburg, PA: Trinity Press, 1997), p. 135, specifically on the overgenerous philanthropy of the emperor, who was to embody the stance of the gods toward the general population. "The relationship proposed by the sacrificial system between god and man …is implicitly offered as a model of the relationship between the elite and the rest of the community."

[104] Later, in chapter 4 of Ephesians, Paul will encourage the readers to be patient with each other as they live worthy of the identity recovered for them through God's grace.

[105] Rodney Stark, *The Rise of Christianity*, pp. 83–84. It is clear from the writings of pagan authors that the Christians outshone their pagan countrymen in caring for others. Stark uses the example of the care given to the sick during periods of disease and epidemic in the Empire.

[106] Thus the edict of Milan establishing tolerance for Christian beliefs in the Empire. In *The Rise of Christianity* (p. 10), Stark estimates that half the population of the Empire would have been Christian by 350 AD, based on the writings of Christians from that era.

[107] This is not a natural paragraph division as determined in Kurt Aland et al., eds., *The Greek New Testament* (New York: United Bible Societies, 1983), p. 669. Nonetheless, I divide the passage here to make it easier to follow the trajectory of Paul's thought in this long paragraph.

[108] I borrow the interpretation of πoιλυποικιλος from Harold K. Moulton, ed., *The Analytical Greek Lexicon Revised* (Grand Rapids: Zondervan, 1977), p. 335.

emperors, senators, governors, proconsuls, magistrates, generals, centurions, and soldiers all fuelling the great Roman machine of the 1ˢᵗ century to bring about peace and security in the Empire. But dreams of a republic gave way to dictatorship as power-hungry leaders sought to devour more land for their own enrichment. The goal was world domination, and in the 1ˢᵗ century AD Rome did dominate the world as the "Babylon"[109] of that day. Peace was clouded by corruption. Hostility toward the Empire was dealt with by violence and execution. Crosses lined the entrances to cities to remind the inhabitants that peace came at the cost of bloodshed: keep your nose clean, stay out of trouble, or you pay with your life. It was a superficial peace, coerced by corporal punishment. Distant nations were kept at bay by wars that won their subjugation as slaves to the Empire. No one dared challenge the authorities if they valued seeing another sunrise in their corner of the great Kingdom of the Caesars.

In this difficult, perilous land, God's community shone like a gold ring on a dirty thumb. Rome could not accomplish peace in Jerusalem, where Jews walked the streets with daggers in their cloaks ready to stab any Gentile[110] who threatened their faith or sacred sites. Yet in these small Christian communities scattered across the cities of the Empire,[111] Jews and Gentiles loved each other. Such a possibility was hard to imagine, yet it was a reality lived out on a daily basis. Wealthy landowner and slave alike gathered[112] in these Christian communities to break bread together, sing together, and read their sacred scriptures and letters from their leaders.[113] Their eagerness to love extended to all; even the cruel figures of the Roman Empire and the exposed babies on the trash heaps outside the

---

[109] I use Babylon as the biblical image representing the ruling worldly power of the day.

[110] N. T. Wright, *The Challenge of Jesus: Rediscovering Who Jesus Was and Is* (Downers Grove, IL: Intervarsity Press, 1999), p.37. Wright describes one of the options chosen by Jews in the early 1ˢᵗ century to rid themselves of Roman Rule: "...the zealot option, that the Sicarii chose who took over Herod's old palace/fortress of Masada during the Roman-Jewish war: say your prayers, sharpen your swords, make yourselves holy to fight holy war, and God will give you a military victory ..."

[111] Rodney Stark, *Cities of God* (San Francisco: Harper, 2006), pp. 76–81. Stark mentions that port cities developed Christian communities sooner than inland cities. He also traces evidence that larger cities in general, as well as cities that were closer to Jerusalem, had Christian communities far sooner than villages and small towns, making early Christianity an urban movement.

[112] Paul's letter to the slave owner, Philemon, suggests that both slave owners and slaves were part of the same community of believers.

[113] In I Corinthians 11:17ff, Paul addresses both wealthy and poor in the church of Corinth. It is apparent that the common meal was shared by rich and poor believers. See Kenneth E. Bailey, *Paul Through Mediterranean Eyes: Cultural Studies in 1 Corinthians* (Downers Grove, IL: IVP Academic, 2011), pp. 318–319: "The poor and the rich were theoretically eating from the same table, and that was good. But being the 'holy temple' and 'the body of Christ' meant (and means) that the community was expected to be transparent, with the pain of each known to all." Cf. Ephesians 5:15–20 for a picture of the early church's worship as a community.

city were objects of love, invited to be part of the community.[114] The common inhabitant of the Empire saw something different in these "Christians."[115] Their actions spoke of a different God, one who was inclusive and loved people.

These actions demonstrated a wisdom and confidence that confounded the rulers and authorities. Nothing like this had been seen before. Members of this community came from every class of Roman society: rich women, landowners, politicians, slaves, servants, children, the elderly.[116] Martyrdom did not stop them. In fact, martyrdom seemed to fuel the fire of their common commitment to the God they served:[117] the more they suffered, the more their community shone with love and acceptance. It was the figure of Jesus that gave them such great faith and confidence. As Paul says, it is the faithfulness of Jesus, in carrying out the work given to Him by the Father, that gives God's community the assurance that His promise will come to fulfillment. These were not perfect communities, but they sought to live according to the principles and structures of a Kingdom that was not yet present except in their commitment to something that could not yet be seen – the final day when God would remove the sceptre of authority and leadership from the present worldly power and give it to the Lord Jesus Christ. Such is the "immense and infinite wisdom of God" in the community of the followers of Christ.[118]

---

[114] Will Durant, *Caesar and Christ: A History of Roman Civilization and of Christianity from their Beginnings to A.D. 325* (New York: Simon and Schuster, 1944), p. 598. "Abortion and infanticide, which were decimating pagan society, were forbidden to Christians as the equivalent of murder; in many instances Christians rescued exposed infants, baptized them, and brought them up with the aid of the community fund."

[115] A derogatory title given to followers of Christ by the Romans. Christians referred to themselves as "people of the Way."

[116] Rodney Stark, *The Rise of Christianity* (San Francisco: Harper, 1997), pp. 30–31. Stark points out that the early Christian community was made up not only of "proletarian" and low-class people, but also of people of means and wealth. In fact, sociological factors suggest that Christianity would have been identified as a "cult" and so found to be attractive to the upper-class and wealthy as well.

[117] Ibid, pp. 172–173. Stark suggests that the perceived eternal compensation of "giving one's life for their faith" became less risky simply because the Christian community "promoted, produced, or consumed collectively" the practice of martyrdom that solidified its belief and practice in the early church period.

[118] N. T. Wright, *Simply Jesus: A New Vision of Who He Was, What He Did, And Why He Matters* (New York: Harper One, 2011), p. 198. According to Wright, the early Christians "…were not ordinary revolutionaries, ready to take up arms to overthrow an existing regime and establish their own instead. Celebrating Jesus as the world's rightful king – as we see them doing in our earliest documents, the letters of Paul – was indeed a way of posing a challenge to Caesar and all other earthy 'lords.' But it was a different sort of challenge. It was not only the announcement of Jesus as the true king, albeit still the king-in-waiting, but that announcement of him as the true *sort* of king." This would be a king who would build his kingdom not through killing and war and violence, but through the establishment of peace.

The wisdom of God present through the work of the Spirit created a community that was unparalleled in the 1ˢᵗ century. Appearing weak and insignificant, this community wielded a hidden power that slowly, over time, wove itself into the fabric of the lives of people in the Empire – so much so that after 300 years, this community included half the Empire's inhabitants and brought an emperor to the conclusion that the God they served was worth serving.[119] No leader had ever accomplished something like this, but God did, in a variety of ways in the lives of a broad spectrum of people.

No other organization, community, or entity exhibited such ability to organize people from all walks of life and levels of society to live out the belief in a loving, caring God who instilled a sense of self-worth in humanity.[120] This community is the creation of a God like no other, a God who demonstrates an "immense and infinite wisdom" far beyond any other ruler, authority, power, or person. It is a community that belongs to Him and that bears the character of Christ, elevating humanity and the rest of creation all around them and replacing the despair of a decaying culture with the hope of a coming Kingdom where love and peace reign.

Ephesians 3:14–19

For all this, I bow on my knees to the Father of our Lord Jesus Christ, from whom every being in heaven and earth finds its identity. [I pray] that from the riches that God is famous for, you may be strengthened in power through His Spirit on the inside so that Christ may live through faith in your heart. This will work to help you be rooted and established in love, so that you are able to grasp with all the holy ones what is the full experience of knowing the awesome greatness of Christ's love, so that you may be filled with all the fullness of [relationship with] God.

STRENGTHENED IN CHRIST BY THE SPIRIT

It was no human power that was generating such a change in people; it was none other than the work of God's Spirit inside men and women. To echo the

---

[119] See Rodney Stark, *Rise of Christianity*, p. 10. He estimates that the population of the Empire in 350 AD was 60 million people, with Christians representing 33 million. This figure is based on a sociological determination that the rate of growth of the Christian community from its inception was 40 percent per decade.

[120] Ibid, p. 200. "Moreover, while people often appealed to various gods for help, it was not assumed that the gods truly cared about humans – Aristotle taught that gods could feel no love for mere humans."

words of Paul in the second half of chapter 1, God goes about changing people from the inside out. What Jesus did on the cross was to bring humanity into the richness of relationship with God, so that the character of His community declares who God is. This character involves a complete reliance on the person of Christ both for faith and for life, and that dependence leads to the continuous pouring of a foundation of love and fellowship both with God and with others. The hope is that the resulting community will grow into the fullness of that loving relationship. Paul's desire for the believers is none other than a complete and utter surrender of themselves to God so that they can experience the depth and breadth of relationship that Christ brings into their lives – that is, full participation in the love of the Father, Son, and Spirit.

One can appreciate the impact of these words of Paul on the believers scattered throughout the Empire. The backdrop is a pantheon of gods claimed by various ethnic groups, all of whom are regarded as suspect by men and women because they profess neither interest nor concern for the general wellbeing of humanity. Most pagans are working at convincing the gods to help them or to do their bidding. But the God that Paul speaks of is not like these. Rather, His character is one of profound love and care for humanity. The sacrifice of Christ, the desire to be involved in the life of His creation, the giving of His Spirit to work inside us, the elimination of hostility, and the gathering of all people together with full access to intimate relationship with Him – all of this is new for people in the Empire.

I worry especially that as God's community today, we have lost the wonder of such a connection and relationship. Our world begs to see a God who cares like the Father Paul is writing about. What it takes to show this wonder to the world around us is a complete abandonment of our person into the hands of this loving God, coupled with a deep understanding – not only in our minds but in our hearts – of what Christ has accomplished for us. Have you felt the full extent of Christ's love in your life? Have you let Him enter in by His Spirit and do the work of making you live again in the kind of life that He desires for each of us? Are we caught by the breadth of His love that reaches into every area of our life and so compels us to live as His loving community?

I think that, all too often, we have succumbed to the temptation to form our own structure and organization that tries to accomplish what only God can do inside us by His Spirit on the foundation Christ has given us. If we want to know what we should look like as God's people, Paul points us to Christ. The faith that Paul speaks of in this section of the letter is none other than a complete trust[121] in the person of Christ. It is not a faith that we generate on our own; it is given to us, and as we see Christ in this faith, which is in fact His own faithfulness, our response is to trust Him completely.

We want God to bless our community, but we falter when we look for that blessing primarily in the growth of our material worth. The richness that God has to give is the strengthening of our inner being, so that we have both a foundation and a resolve to be what God has created us to be. There are echoes here of chapter 2 and our creation as God's masterpieces, living in harmony with God and His creation so as to cause that creation to flourish in the economy He has prepared for it. This growth, as Paul knows all too well, is the most valuable evidence of God's riches (hence *Spiritual blessings*) among us. As human beings we are at our best when we are rooted in such a relationship, living out of such an identity. At the beginning of chapter 4, Paul will emphasize the need for patience with each other so that we may all grow into the desired character and life of this community. I am confident that we are all in the continuous process of letting the Spirit develop us into the people God desires us to be; the hope is that we will let Him lead us into a fuller experience of the extreme love of the Father, Son, and Spirit for humanity and creation.

Ephesians 3:20–21

Now to Him who is capable of doing outrageously more than we could ever ask for or think of, in keeping with the power that works in us, to Him goes all the fame and the honour in God's community and in Jesus Christ to all people throughout all the ages, Amen.

MORE THAN WE CAN EVER IMAGINE

Keeping the focus on what Christ has accomplished and the power of God working in us, Paul now establishes the full scope of possibility if we let God truly transform us in our inner being. The result is out of this world! When we

---

[121] The word Paul uses is πιστεως, genitive singular of πιστις, from the root word πειθω, meaning "trust." For a full explanation see Colin Brown, ed., *The New International Dictionary of New Testament Theology*, vol. 1 (Grand Rapids, IL: Zondervan, 1975), p. 588. According to Brown, the two Hebrew words offering a background for the use of the Greek word πιστις in the New Testament are *aman*, meaning "be true or reliable" and *batah*, meaning "to trust, rely upon." These two aspects, faith and faithfulness, merge into an eschatological sense of "hope" in Paul's usage of πιστις, where faith is an expectation based on the reliability of who God is and what He has done or has to offer (see p. 601). Paul desires that Christ be present in His people through faith, and that faith will lead them to the end goal of experiencing the full extent of relationship in the triune community.

let God do what He wants in us, in order to shape us into the desired creation Paul has already spoken of in chapters 1 and 2, He will surpass all anticipation. Think of the most eagerly anticipated events in life: our first words, our first solo bike ride without the training wheels, our graduation day, landing our first job, getting our first paycheque, that first time behind the wheel on our own, falling in love with the one we will spend our life with, the birth of our children, realizing a dream, accomplishing that one thing that we have worked for all our life! God can do far more than that if we let Him work in us at the depth of relationship He desires!

God can do so much more, in fact, that Paul uses a superlative on top of a superlative to make his point.[122] If we allow God to work in us through relationship, so that we experience the full extent of the love and fellowship that exist among the Father, Son, and Spirit, the possibilities are beyond comprehension. What God will do is greater than anything we can ever imagine or even think to ask of Him. We will always come up short in asking Him for this, because even the most creative and adventurous cannot possibly think to ask God for what He actually truly wants for us.

Unlike the selfish gods of the pagan pantheon, the Father who gives us all the riches of heaven will do more than we could ever plan for. It is impossible to out-imagine, outthink, or outdo God. We can have the most dynamic, all-encompassing plan, with the fullest of expectations, and God will still do more than that! As a pastor, hindsight has always shown me that while God is doing something in the life of one person, He is simultaneously connecting endless possibilities for impact in the lives of others, and vice versa. There is no matching His ability or perspective. If we simply let Him do the work in us, so that we live in the unity and peace that comes by the work of Christ and the work of the Spirit in us both individually and corporately, we will continue to be the community that can change an Empire and the world.

This God warrants not only our attention but also our love and our honour and our praise. He must at all times be the centre of our community as God's people. He is the Giver, Sustainer, Redeemer, Creator, and loving Father who weaves the fabric of His creation to reflect His love and relationality. Everywhere you look, His hands have been there. He is famous for giving and redeeming, and Paul wants to remind us that He is famous for doing outrageously more than we could ever imagine. This is our God! All praise and honour and fame

---

[122] Paul takes the adverb περισσῶς, meaning "superabundantly", and puts ὑπερ in front of it to add "super" to the superlative! In my translation I have used the word "outrageously" to convey this.

go to Him! The reality that Jews and Gentiles were actually living in community together, loving one another, was proof to Paul and to the early believers that not only was this God serious about fulfilling His promise to bless humanity, but He had the power to produce the completely unexpected! In Christ, through the Spirit, God the Father has created the condition for the most connected and fulfilling community possible.

In the chapters now remaining, Paul will begin describing what such a community looks like when it puts all its trust in God, and what its ultimate goal is in God's plan for the whole world.

Chapter Six

UNITY IN DIVERSITY

Ephesians 4:1–10

In light of all this I, who am in chains for the Lord, beg you to live a life comparable to the life you have been called to live [by God] and to live in it with all humility and gentleness [and] with patience, putting up with one another in love. Be diligent in maintaining the unity that comes from the Spirit, together with peace. There is one Body and one Spirit, just as you were called to live in the life centered on one hope;[123] one Lord, one faith, one baptism, one God and Father of all, who is over all and through all and in all. But to each one of us was given grace in relation to the measure of Christ's gift.[124] Consequently the Psalmist said,

When he ascended on high he led those from captivity to freedom[125] and gave gifts to men.

What did "he ascended" mean except that he also descended into the lower region of the earth? He who descended is the one who ascended far above the heavens, that he might fill all things.

ONE GOD, ONE PEOPLE

Paul now reaches a pivotal transition in the letter, taking the focus from revelation to application. After having talked about what it is that God has done in terms of his plan for creation and the human race, he now lays out how God's community should respond to this revelation. This is similar to what we see

---

[123] Paul makes a play on the words παρακαλω and καλεω in this section, both containing the root meaning "call". He does so to exaggerate the point that, given what he has described in the first three chapters regarding the life that God has obtained for us in Christ, the readers are now to go and live out that life as a community. I have tried to keep that point explicit, especially here, by translating εν as "on" rather than "in": this is to remain consistent with the theme presented so far and further developed in this passage, that the "hope" set out in Paul's picture of God and His plan is our *foundation* and our *focus* for living.

[124] For της δωρεας του Χριστου I am following the RSV translation, "Christ's gift", as it makes clear the source from which grace is measured out to us.

[125] I chose to translate the phrase "captive captivity" as "from captivity to freedom" to show Paul's intent in using this Psalm to clarify the point he is making in this passage. I will say more on this in the following pages.

in his letter to the Roman believers at the beginning of Romans 12.[126] Whereas in Romans he addresses the personal response of believers, which is to give their lives as "living sacrifices" to a God who does not condemn humanity but desires to restore men and women to relationship with Him, here Paul addresses the community and bids them to live collectively the life they were given by God to live. In Romans the focus is on giving oneself to God in light of all that He has done for us. In Ephesians the focus is on living together out of the amazing story revealed to us as reality and brought to its climax in Jesus.

The play on the root word "call" in the first verse[127] gives force to Paul's exhortation to the readers to live in a way that reflects the true story which God has revealed to us and in which we are participants with Him. In that story God is creating one new humanity in Christ, and in that humanity we are to live in loving relationship with God – Father, Son, and Spirit – and with one another. Paul will now paint the picture of what it looks like to "live with others in light of our relationship with God" as His community, focused on Christ.

I love the realism of Paul's directive in verse 2 about being patient with each other. It would be all too easy for some, emerging from the first three chapters of the letter with the big picture of what God is up to in our life and in our world, to demand full and instant compliance from those around them. For Paul, it is much more organic than that. The focus is literally on how we "walk."[128] Walking is a daily occurrence, and it implies progress along a path. To live in keeping with the goal and purpose to which God has called us (clearly spelled out in the first three chapters) will take great patience and a character of humility and gentleness, putting up with our collective struggle to be God's community. The struggle is essentially the privilege of "hammering"[129] out what we are to be as we live with each other and engage those who are outside the community.

---

[126] F. F. Bruce, *The New International Commentary on the New Testament: The Epistles to the Colossians, to Philemon, and to the Ephesians* (Grand Rapids, MI: Eerdmans, 1984), p. 333. "As in other Pauline letters, the doctrine expounded in the earlier part is to be worked out according to the practical guidance given in the later part, the transition from the one to the other being marked by the adverb 'therefore.'" I find this an important indicator of authorship in that it shows continuity between Ephesians and the other writings attributed to Paul by the greater scholarly community.

[127] Literally Paul writes, "I call on you to live according to the calling with which you were called."

[128] That is the literal translation of περιπατεω, which I've chosen to render as "live", our closest contemporary equivalent as explained earlier. In fact, the theme of application to life can be traced by Paul's frequent use of the word in the remaining three chapters: in 4:1, 4:17, 5:2, 5:8, and 5:15.

[129] "Hammering" is the appropriate word here; I envision us as a piece of metal in a blacksmith's forge, being softened by the extreme heat of the coals and then hammered into shape, only to be put back into the fire and brought through the whole process again, each time closer to the blacksmith's design. Watching a blacksmith at work makes this picture vivid.

The reality is that God's community is not perfect – at least, not in the sense that they "have it all together".[130] Sometimes certain individuals will struggle. In fact, it's safe to say that at some point or other everyone will struggle to attain to what the community is called to be; certainly a reading of Paul's other twelve letters bear that out. Paul knows that the community has not "arrived", but he urges the readers to work continually toward the goal, being patient with one another as each one learns to let the Spirit work within them and tries to live in His power the life that God desires. This entails kindness and latitude toward each other as we grow into what God desires each of us to be.[131]

The focus and foundation of behaviour as God's community is love. Paul makes this clear to the believers in Galatia when he reminds them that what matters in God's community is "faith working through love".[132] The latitude we allow each other in this community is based on our trust in Christ that He will work in us by His Spirit to make us what the Father desires us to be. In other words, because we are confident of His power to complete the work in us, we can afford to be patient and merciful with one another and allow time for the process. As we trust, we are to go about loving each other; this means focusing always on *what we will become* rather than on *what we have done*.

All too often we tend to get caught up in what we've done. Looking at the past will only show us a pattern of getting it right some of the time, interspersed with moments where we stumble, only to get up and go at it again with a goal of improving our focus and behaviour. The process repeats itself. It is far better to stay eschatologically focused: knowing what God wants us to be, and what we *will* be by His grace, we work on a daily basis to participate with Him and move into that future together, trusting that God is doing the work in each one of us by His Spirit as we go about loving one another. The Spirit is key

---

[130] N. T. Wright, *The New Testament and the People of God* (Minneapolis: Fortress, 1992), p. 452: "A 'pure' period, when everyone believed exactly the same thing, lived in a community without problems or quarrels, and hammered out True Doctrine for the coming Great Church, never existed. It is, perhaps, important to point out that the author of Acts would be happy to say: I told you so." Wright goes on to enumerate the issues in Acts, about which Luke writes quite openly, that gave rise to problems, quarrels, and disagreements right from the beginning.

[131] See Gordon Fee, *God's Empowering Presence*, p. 724. Fee points out the "already/not yet" reality of Christ's victory over evil among God's people. "As with their redemption in Christ, which, evidenced by the Spirit's presence, is 'already' but 'not yet,' so too with Christ's triumph over the powers. It is 'already' so they themselves must…be aware that the conflict goes on…"

[132] N. T. Wright, *The Kingdom New Testament: A Contemporary Translation* (New York: HarperOne, 2011), p. 388.

to keeping our eyes on the goal and enabling us to love. That is the kind of community Paul is encouraging the readers to be.[133]

Paul then points to the fabric that constitutes and maintains the unity in this community. True unity is maintained by the Spirit when we let Him lead. The Spirit's intent is to shape us more and more into the character of Christ[134] – the new, true humanity. This is the only way that the community can maintain peace; as soon as it strays from this focus, it lets the hostility of fallen humanity back in all over again, and creates rifts and fractured relationships. As a Pentecostal, I've seen too much glib declaration of the Spirit's presence while God's community is fractured by hostility and severed relationship.[135] Unity that comes by the Spirit creates a community focused on trusting God while loving each other. Will there still be some struggle? Yes. But the struggle will not overpower the unity in the community and the love its people have for one another; rather, struggle will evoke the response of love and will be the occasion of mutual encouragement.

The focus should be on continually letting the Spirit work to change us from the inside out. If we neglect this, we will tend to become preoccupied with changing the outside in order to effect a change within. And when a community is preoccupied with the outside, a superficiality sets in that undermines the foundation of love and creates all kinds of strife for the community. We see this in Paul's letters to the Romans and Corinthians, where believers were putting stock in outward things such as nationality, ethnicity, social class, sensational experience, and visible charismatic manifestations while ignoring the work of the Spirit necessary to establish the wholeness they needed to live in harmony and unity.

---

[133] See N. T. Wright, *The New Testament and the People of God*, pp. 460–461. Wright mentions the hope of the early church in Jesus' phrase, "on earth as it is in heaven." Jesus' resurrection indicated that the hope of future resurrection is certain. Plodding along and working at becoming the community God desires, we have always before us the future hope of completion. "[T]he Christians believed that Israel's god, being the creator, would physically recreate those who were his own, at some time and in some space the other side of death. New, bodily human beings will require a new world in which to live. In the transformed world order, the veil will be lifted for all time. The realities of the heavenly world will be visibly united with the realities of the earthly."

[134] Cf. Ephesians 3:14–19.

[135] I have also seen, in that same Pentecostal context, what happens when God's community focuses on Christ and lives by the Spirit. There is nothing like it in any other organization on earth. Some in my circle of family and friends have shared experiences that closely approximate this in twelve-step groups such as Alcoholics Anonymous.

Paul then moves into confirming the foundation of this community: one faith that has one Spirit, one Lord, one God,[136] and one hope that comes from relationship with the triune God – namely, the hope of a new humanity.[137] This running theme of "one" in verses 4–6 places God's community on a foundational relationship to the only true God, who reveals Himself through Christ. "One God and one Lord" is an identifying statement of uniqueness in contradistinction to the paganism of the Empire.[138] As opposed to many gods, this faith is built on one God; as opposed to many lords, this faith is based on one Lord. The unity of God's community is grounded in the unity of the triune God in whom it trusts.[139] It is also possible, given that Ephesians is a general letter, that Paul is referring not only to unity within a local church but to unity among and between the churches.[140]

Pivotal to this unity is the one Father who is over all, through all, and in all.[141] These words pick up the theme woven throughout the letter, of the God who reveals Himself as Father and who wills that the world and humanity receive the richness of relationship with Him. He is "over all": His character, as the one "who marks out beforehand" the plan that will secure His relationship to humanity and provide a way of redemption and renewal for the world and the human race, reveals His providence, sustaining power, and will over the creation.

---

[136] F. F. Bruce, *The Epistle to the Colossians to Philemon and to the Ephesians The New International Commentary on the New Testament*, pp. 337–338. Bruce points out that this pattern of "one Spirit, one Lord, one God" is repeated in varying forms in 1 Corinthians 8:6 and 1 Corinthians 12:13 – specifically repeating "one Body and one Spirit" –which lends support to the belief that this is an early church "credo" or confession of faith.

[137] In Romans 8 Paul takes this a step further, pointing out that a new humanity will also translate into a new creation – by which he means the earth.

[138] N. T. Wright, *The New Testament and the People of God*, p. 450. "What we seem to be faced with is the existence of a community which was perceived to be subverting the normal social and cultural life of the empire precisely by its quasi-familial, quasi-ethnic life as a community. It was a new family, a 'third race', neither Jew nor Gentile but 'in Christ.'"

[139] Colin E. Gunton, *The Christian Faith* (Oxford, UK: Blackwell, 2002), p. 186: "God is not a monad – God is not lonely, as some of the early theologians said – because communion is intrinsic to his being. If we ask how three can be one, the answer is that this God is one only by virtue of the way in which Father, Son, and Spirit mutually and reciprocally give to and receive from each other everything that they are. – God is only what he is as three persons whose being is so closely bound up with one another that they together constitute one God."

[140] John Stott, *The Bible Speaks Today: The Message of Ephesians* (Downers Grove, IL: Intervarsity Press, 1979), p. 154.

[141] There is no multi-denominational reference by Paul here. His focus is on the difference between this God and His story with humanity, on the one hand, and the pagan gods on the other. There is no splintering of the church into Catholic, Anglican, Orthodox, and Protestant. What this emphasis should tell us is how unified the church was in its infancy, with its leaders always intending that they all be one, however scattered in the Empire.

Paul is also, in this phrase, emphasizing the Father's continual attentive, hovering presence, a reality that is noticeable from the first page of Genesis; the long line of narrative from that moment on is filled with the desire of this Father to dwell with His creation. The phrase "through all" points to how, by His Spirit, He embeds His character into our lives so that we live as His community, showing forth who He essentially is in His being.[142] And the "in all" is the reality that all creation is connected to Him; He is active everywhere, holding everything together, and evidence of who He is presents itself in every aspect of creation. This is not a pantheistic[143] statement, but a comment on the relationship of "in" that speaks of the most intimate of connection with His creation.[144]

What is clear up to this point in the chapter is that God's community is unified by being founded and focused on God Himself, through the ongoing work of His Spirit who establishes peace within the community and leads its participants into the new humanity that God desires. Now Paul will shift to commenting on the necessary *diversity* that characterizes the unity in this community. But before speaking of the character of that diversity, he focuses on the fact that all have received God's grace in relation to the measure of Christ's gift of Himself. What is this measure? It is unlimited, for this total giving of Himself, and the fruit thereof, is none other than a restoration of our humanity to relationship with the one true God: Father, Son, and Spirit.

To make this clear, Paul quotes a verse from Psalm 68. In this psalm, the psalmist speaks of Israel's God who frees His people from their enemies. The psalm recalls the Exodus narrative and the coming of God on Mount Sinai, descending into the Israelite camp and dwelling with His people. It speaks of God as "Father to the fatherless"[145] and declares, "Our God is a God who saves! The Sovereign LORD rescues us from death."[146] Paul borrows the theme of this psalm and applies it to Christ. What Jesus does in His mission of rescuing

---

[142] What we show forth is the unity of relationship we share as God's community, which mirrors the unity shared by Father, Son, and Spirit.

[143] There is no notion here of the divine essence indwelling or permeating all things, as in a Buddhist understanding. Paul's language refers not to *substance* but to *relationship*.

[144] John in his gospel (14:20) makes this clear by the language that Jesus uses in His evening discourse to His disciples at the last meal. "When I am raised again, you will know that I am in my Father, and you are in me, and I am in you" (NLT). He shares the heart of the Father with them as He expresses both His and the Father's will to "abide" in them. This use of "in" is very distinct from our common use of "with" when we speak of being together. The Father does more than just be "with"; he delves much more deeply into relationship and speaks of being "in."

[145] Cf. Psalm 68:5. "Father to the fatherless, defender of widows – this is God, whose dwelling is holy. God places the lonely in families; he sets the prisoners free and gives them joy" (NLT).

[146] Psalm 68:20 (NLT).

humanity through His death and resurrection is in keeping with the character of God as drawn by the psalmist in the story of Israel. Christ descends and steps into the human condition in order to redeem it so that relationship can continue. This is exactly what God did in the Exodus narrative, descending from Mount Sinai and dwelling with His people, making it possible for them to have relationship with Him.[147]

The other parallel suggested by Paul's quotation of this psalm is Moses and Christ. Like Moses, who ascended to Mount Sinai and brought back the Torah, Jesus ascended to the Father and has descended again in the Spirit, bringing the gift of freedom from sin and death. It is by the Spirit that Christ returns to dwell with humanity following His ascension, particularly in His community, and by the Spirit He gives all kinds of gifts to each person as outlined already in the letter.[148]

In the above parallel, ascending comes *before* descending. But Paul gives another meaning to Christ's "descending" by adding "into the lower region of the earth". There is a variety of opinion as to what Paul means here, but it can safely be assumed that the words "into the lower region of the earth" relate to Christ's death and burial, which are in turn *followed by* His resurrection and ascension. In conjunction with the image of the release of captives, borrowed from Psalm 68, some interpret this passage to suggest that Christ entered Hades and released the faithful who were captive there. Others view it as Jesus experiencing the full extent of alienation through death, as all humans experience it, in order to then free humanity from such alienation.[149] Whatever Paul intends here, it must be in keeping with the greater idea he is conveying, that Christ's gift of Himself to humanity has resulted in grace being measured out to us now in the same measure as the sacrifice in which He gave it by His death and resurrection.

We have been given grace through what Christ has done for us, and His death and resurrection describes the "measure" by which it was given. The extent of this "measure" is new life – the life of Christ Himself – and our being "seated

---

[147] The sacrificial system, incorporated into the tabernacle worship, gave Israelites the opportunity to connect with God through sacrifice.

[148] N. T. Wright, *Paul for Everyone: Prison Letters* (Louisville, KY: Westminster John Knox Press, 2004) EPub File, pp. 130–131. "In line with several early Christian writings, Paul sees the ascension of Jesus as being in a sense like that of Moses. After the 'new Exodus' which had been achieved in his death and resurrection, setting the human race free from bondage to sin and death, Jesus 'went up' into the heavenly realm where he now reigns as Lord. Instead of coming down again with the law, as Moses had done, Jesus 'returned' in the person of the Spirit, through whom different gifts are now showered on the church."

[149] John Stott, *The Bible Speaks Today: The Message of Ephesians*, pp. 158–159. Stott gives a good summation of the various interpretations of what Paul means by "the lower regions of the earth".

in the heavenly realms in Christ Jesus", as Paul declared earlier in 2:6.[150] The significance of this is related to the connection that each believer has with Christ: the gift God gives us in Christ, who is both the true human and God the Son, is none other than to be able to live out of the depth of relationship that He enjoys with the Father and Spirit. In this sense there is a present as well as an eschatological focus: we know that what we have now, we will have in full later because of the measure of the gift of Christ.

A parallel passage is found in Romans 12:3–6, where Paul uses the word "measure" in relation to the diversity given to each believer based on the grace given to all. In this passage, Paul points out that all should have a humble self-reflection regarding their place in God's community based on the "measure of faith" God has given to each. The point here is that the "measure of faith" has its source in God through Christ, and not through the individual's own ability to "believe" and "trust". The problem Paul was addressing in the Roman letter was that the believers in that church had taken to measuring each other according to their individual faith. Paul reminds them to reassess themselves as God's community according to the faith given by Christ. This causes all to realize the unity and equality in which they live as God's people. Paul then qualifies this "measure" again in verse 6 by stating that each has gifts that are different; *different gifts* based on the *same grace* given by God.[151]

Back now to Ephesians 4, where Paul is affirming that in God's community, God gives grace in the measure of the gift that Christ has given, so that each experiences the fullness of what God desires for them. That fullness will come not in the capacity of individuals to attain it for themselves, but through the diverse roles they will play as each lives out, with the others, the fullness of Christ's gift; the individual element is the uniqueness that each one brings to the community, but the fullness is being achieved by the Spirit working in each one and in the community as a whole. It is in this way that Christ "fills" all things. Again, this idea of "filling" is not a pantheistic one, but one that evokes the relational connection God has with His creation. Our connection to the Father through Christ is continued through the work of the Spirit, so that we become the community God desires us to be. In this community, participating in the work of the Spirit in us, we strive to live in the fullness of relationship with God, with each other, and with those in the world in the same way that God Himself does in His trinitarian relationship.

---

[150] Robert H. Gundry, *Commentary on Ephesians*, (Baker Academic, 2010; EPub file), p. 111.
[151] In Romans 12:6 the adjective διαφορα modifies χαρισματα not χαριν.

Ephesians 4:11–16

[The gifts] he gave [were that] some be apostles, some prophets, some evangelists, some pastors and teachers, for preparing the holy ones for the work of serving to build up the body of Christ until we arrive at being one[152] in the faith and one in the knowledge of the Son of God toward full-grown manhood. The measure of this manhood is maturity [that comes] from the fullness of Christ. [The point of this] is that we no longer be like children tossed around and led astray by every new teaching that appears from deceptive men who seek to trick others with their craftiness and seduce them with error. But by speaking the truth in love, we may be grown-up in everything in Him who is the leader, Christ! From Him all the body [is] well fitted and put together so that every piece works according to the measure of its individual part and so makes the body increase by building itself up in love.

MIRRORING FOR THE WORLD WHAT GOD DESIRES

Having identified the measure of the gift that Christ gives, Paul now talks about the diversity created by specific gifts, a diversity that will maintain the oneness and unity God desires for His community. Those gifts have to do with the type of leadership God has designed in order to enable the community to function as His loving people. This part of Paul's letter shows what kind of leadership causes that community to thrive.

In the culture of Paul's day (and in what human culture is this not the tendency?), leaders took from the people. In order to exert their leadership, they took money, power, influence, territory, and the right of self-government away from people[153] and used these things to wield power in the Empire. The Roman Empire was an oligarchy: the wealthy few ruled, while the great mass of the poor and the middle class served the egos and ambitions of the rich.[154] But in God's community, the leader, Christ, gives gifts to the people. This leader gives of His

---

[152] The common translation of ενοτης is "unity." I've decided to translate it as "one" to capitalize on the theme of "one" running through the letter – especially that of one new humanity.

[153] In Jeffrey A. Winters' work, *Oligarchy* (Cambridge University Press, 2011; EPub file), he describes the practice of *Latifundia* among the wealthy of the Empire during the last 400 years BCE, where they bought up thousands of acres of land and so created a monopoly that allowed them to exert inordinate influence and power as a demographic, single-handedly controlling the Empire. During the first 100 years of the Common Era, certain oligarchs begin adapting the rule of "proscription" in order to subdue and eliminate any competing oligarchs who did not side with their political goals. See Winters' chapter on Rome for a brilliant explanation of this social construct in the Roman Empire.

[154] Ibid., p. 90: "At the top of the system were the rich and ultra-rich. From there the drop-off was steep for the tens of millions of poor and landless below."

wealth instead of amassing wealth by taking from others. In the same way, the gift of leadership to some individuals is given not to serve ambition and inflate egos, but to enable the community to build itself up, to prepare the community to be what God desires. God's desire is that the community's leaders help it to grow in its capacity to live as a unified group of men and women who believe the one faith and trust the one God that Paul mentioned earlier – and more specifically, to be of one mind in their understanding of who Jesus is as the Son of God. For Paul, understanding the role and significance of the person of Christ is pivotal to the community's focus and purpose as well as its growth.[155]

Leadership should bring about maturity, "full manhood", in God's community. The character of each leadership office adds a maturing element to the varied dynamic of the community. *Apostles* allow the church to expand as they strike out and found new communities, all the while upholding the faith and belief of the community as a whole.[156] *Prophets* remind the community of God's purposes from a cosmic perspective, so that the community does not get side-tracked by other issues.[157] *Evangelists* continue to tell the story of God's plan for the world, so that others may know it and join God's community. *Pastors* shepherd the community through their ministry of presence, so that the community feels cared for, prayed for, and protected. *Teachers* carry on the instruction in God's word, so that the community continues to develop in its knowledge of God's character and its understanding of who they are called to be in light of their relationship with Him.

When these leadership roles are functioning in the church, and those occupying them give from the measure of the gift of Christ given to them, then the community is built up. The moment any one of these individual leaders succumbs to the culture and begins to usurp the authority given to them by Christ, serving their own ambition and ego instead of their fellow believers, or holding back their gift, the community suffers. A community functioning in the way God desires is one that has leaders who give in such a way that complements what the other leaders give, so that unity and oneness is maintained in the

---

[155] John Stott, *The Bible Speaks Today: The Message of Ephesians*, pp. 169–170. "And the unity to which we are to come one day is that full unity which a full faith in and knowledge of the Son of God will make possible. This expression effectively disposes of the argument that unity can grow without faith or knowledge. On the contrary, it is precisely the more we know and trust the Son of God that we grow in the kind of unity with one another which he desires."

[156] I take the Apostle Paul himself as an example of the function of this leadership office in the church.

[157] Paul is not inventing a New Testament model for prophet; rather, he builds on the role of prophet as "covenant enforcement mediators" in the Old Testament. Prophets remind God's people of what God's plan is and what their place is in that plan.

community. One of the mistakes often made by leaders is that they exclude or detach themselves from the community in such a way that they neglect their own growth. The reality is that as they take up their leadership and give, enfolded in the community along with other leaders, they too will grow and be built up. They need the leadership of other leaders for their own growth and preparation for service. No leader has "arrived" so as to be without need for further growth; only Christ holds that kind of leadership role in God's community.[158]

Measuring the degree of "growing up"[159] in a community comes by matching that growth against the fullness of maturity that exists in Christ. The characteristics of that fullness can be derived from some of the things Paul has already said in the letter. Is God viewed as Father, who desires to give the richness of His Spirit to His creation (1:3–7)? Is there a love for people everywhere (1:15, 2:13)? Is there a humility that does not boast in itself but boasts in God (2:9)? Does humanity function in the community by making the creation a better place (2:10)? Is faith and belief in the community inclusive (2:15)?[160] Is there evidence of reconciliation (2:16)? Is there peace and harmony (2: 15)? Does the community share the news of peace with others (2:17)? Is there focus on belonging and acceptance in the community (2:19–22)? Is everyone viewed as equal (3:6)? Do the least deserving have a prominent place in the community (3:8)? Do earthly authorities respond in awe and admiration at the community's countercultural activity and influence (3:10)? Is there an ongoing openness and cultivation of God's presence in the community (3:12)? Is the Holy Spirit evident and present (3:16)? Do individuals in the community exhibit an incredible inner strength in the face of challenge and difficulty (3:16–17)? Is the depth and breadth of God's love tested and increasingly acted upon from day to day (3:18)? Does the community have an attitude of expecting more than it can ever imagine or think of (3:20–21)? This is a sampling of the potential signs of maturity that Paul describes in Ephesians alone based on the person and character of Christ.

---

[158] Jim Herrington et al., *The Leader's Journey: Accepting the Call to Personal and Congregational Transformation* (San Francisco: Jossey-Bass, 2003), p. 157: "Not many of us can accomplish the task of transformation by working alone. Yielding our lives to Jesus Christ and walking with a community of fellow learners is essential." This book has helped me see the gift God gives to leaders, of working *with their communities* toward transformation, so that as the community grows, so does the leader. Communities where both leaders and people grow are strong.

[159] F. F. Bruce, *The Epistles to the Colossians, to Philemon, and to the Ephesians*, pp. 349–350. Bruce explains that ανδρα τελειον, which can be translated "perfect man", does not have the sense it would have in gnostic belief, of having arrived at a state of flawlessness. Rather, it is a term used by Paul to indicate maturity. "The new humanity on earth, it is here emphasized, must grow up to adult maturity in order to resist all the adverse forces that threaten its health and effectiveness."

[160] In other words, is everyone welcome to participate in the one faith as Paul describes it in chapter 4?

We need to continually take the measure of maturity in our communities on all of these fronts. If we lack maturity, one way of taking a step toward it is to put the necessary elements in place and cultivate the necessary environment. If leadership is lacking, then the mature step is to find and commission appropriate leaders and cultivate an ethic of servant leadership. If focus is lacking, if we have diverted our eyes from Christ, then leaders must make the necessary changes to get the community focused back on Christ. Part of being mature is making the hard corrective decisions that are needed to keep the community on the road toward maturity. Otherwise, as Paul indicates, we will continue to live as children, attending to what satisfies our immediate whim without regard for our calling or responsibility to the community, and it will not grow.

Sometimes growth hurts. Like pains in a child's body from the expansion of joints that shift to accommodate growth, so at times pain will be felt in the community because of the phase of growth it is in. That pain is necessary; without it we cannot grow. Without the suffering of living as a righteous human in a corrupt world, and without the cross, Christ could not have released us from bondage to sin and death. God was willing to take that pain on Himself to make us what we were meant to be, and we are mature in Christ when we are willing to accept pain for the same cause. This is no better realized than when, out of love for God and His people, we acknowledge the reality that we must change, even if it means walking a painful path to reach the goal.

One necessary function of maturity is to prevent the community from being led astray. Paul indicates that continuing as children will make the community vulnerable to anyone with a smoke-and-mirrors show, anyone who can cleverly obscure the truth and so undermine stability. The analogy Paul uses is of children in a boat on the high seas. Being lighter and less experienced, they are readily tossed around, in contrast to the adults on board who have more experience, greater knowledge of how to move around on a boat so as to use their weight to advantage, better navigational skills, and so on. Communities that are easily swayed or manipulated by those who want to profit from them are not mature. They easily get tossed around. They lack the necessary foundation to stand firm and withstand such deception. There are plenty of crafty people who, under the influence of evil, would like to get their hands on the community and hurt God's people; the evil one wants nothing more than for God's community to be weak and vulnerable, since in this state it has absolutely no power or influence on others and so frustrates what God desires to accomplish through it for the world. God desires His people to join Him in the battle against evil. A divided, unstable community cannot battle evil. A mature community whose foundation is secure, that knows the truth and uses it to expose falsehood, is a community that can join God in battling evil.[161]

Paul also mentions that a sign of maturity in God's community is "speaking the truth in love." Having the capacity to confront the truth, engage the truth, and share the truth in a way that conveys love is evidence of a strong, mature community. It takes a lot of teaching, a lot of "patience", a lot of "putting up with each other" to develop into the kind of community that can speak the truth in love. When we think of the characteristics of love listed by Paul in 1 Corinthians 13,[162] we know that it will make for a maturity not readily seen in the surrounding culture – certainly not in the culture of the Roman Empire in the 1st century. When one takes a look at Roman culture as described in earlier chapters of this book, one realizes the resounding difference God's community made in the Empire when they were living out of an atmosphere of love. No wonder Paul says in Romans that "we should be decent and true in everything we do."[163] Simple decency and honesty were absent in the culture of the Empire. In the classical stories of the pagan religions of Rome, the gods "did wicked things to humans – often for the sport of it."[164] This perpetuated a level of irreverence and rudeness and treacherousness in the culture that lowered the sense of decency. Christians, by contrast, served a God who could be trusted, who cherished and cared for people, and that sentiment proved influential as believers then expressed the same caring toward each other and toward all residents of the Empire.

Paul makes his next point by means of an analogy similar to those he uses in other letters. Looking at God's community as a living organism,[165] Paul addresses the relationship of God's people to Christ in a relational structure where Christ is the head. The "growing up" depends on acknowledging who Christ is: the head of the body. The "in him" signifies that the "growing up" can only happen when

---

[161] As we will see, in chapter 6 of Ephesians Paul declares God's desire for a unified community to whom He gives the invitation of joining Him in battling evil. Cf. Romans 12:21: "Don't let evil get the best of you, but conquer evil by doing good" (NLT).

[162] "Love is patient, love is kind. Love is not jealous or boastful or proud or rude. Love does not demand its own way. Love is not irritable, and it keeps no record of when it has been wronged. It is never glad about injustice but rejoices whenever the truth wins out. Love never gives up, never loses faith, is always hopeful, and endures through every circumstance" (1 Cor 13:4–7).

[163] Romans 13:13a (NLT).

[164] Rodney Stark, *The Rise of Christianity*, pp. 200–201.

[165] John Stott, *The Bible Speaks Today: The Message of Ephesians*, p. 171. Take note of Stott's warning in applying the analogy: "We must not look in these verses for inspired instruction on human anatomy and physiology. The apostle's intention is not to teach us how the human body works, but rather how the body of Christ works."

the body is connected to the head. The body that is God's community takes its direction from the head, and its growth is orchestrated by the head. From the top down, the body is fitted and put together in a way that allows for necessary connection and maximum participation, in order for the body to function as its Creator intended.[166] One can see how destructive it is when a leader takes the place of the head who is Christ; there is no way a community can function when a leader is taking the place that can only be occupied by Christ. Only when Jesus is the head does the organism function as it should, and according to Paul the evidence of proper function is growth – the community becoming more and more like Christ.

Paul indicates that each member (joint, ligament, or other part, in keeping with the analogy) "works according to the measure of its individual part". This "measure" is the particular gift or gifts given by the Spirit to enable the individual member to perform an essential supportive function for the sake of the whole body. As every member functions by using and contributing the gifts that it has, the community is built up. Robert H. Gundry, in his commentary on Ephesians, unpacks this quite well:

> "Through every supportive connection" has to do with Christians' sticking together for the purpose of mutual support. "In accordance with the working…of each individual [body] part" puts every Christian to work in a mutually supportive role. "In measure" suits the work of each one to his or her Spiritual gift. Thus "all the body …causes the body's growth for the building up of itself." But the body can do so only by virtue of being fitted together and compacted together by Christ. The building up of itself "in love" recalls speaking the truth "in love" and indicates not only that love for one another should imbue "the working in measure of each individual [body] part" but also that love consists in such work.[167]

A parallel Pauline passage that resonates with verse 16 is found in Romans 12:3–8, where Paul also identifies the organic structure of the body of Christ and the importance of each member's participation for the wholeness of the community. The passage immediately precedes instruction regarding the

---

[166] N. T. Wright, *Paul for Everyone: Prison Letters*, p. 146. "Every Christian, equipped by God to play his or her part within the whole community, has a role in enabling the body to function as the complex and interdependent entity that it is. And all, we note once more, must be done in love."
[167] Robert H. Gundry, *Commentary on Ephesians*, pp. 63–67.

need for genuine love: not just "pretending to love others" but "really loving others."[168]

Love has a two-way function in the community. Each member *receives* love from the others, which motivates and encourages him to live out his gift; in turn, by using his gift for the community's benefit, each member *expresses* the same love to the others. It is this continuous mutual exchange of love that causes growth. In Colossians 2, Paul writes about the kind of behaviour that arises when a community's members do not operate out of love:

So don't let anyone condemn you for what you eat or drink, or for not celebrating certain holy days or new-moon ceremonies or Sabbaths. For these rules were only shadows of the real thing, Christ himself. Don't let anyone condemn you by insisting on self-denial. And don't let anyone say you must worship angels, even though they say they have visions about this. These people claim to be so humble, but their sinful minds have made them proud. But they are not connected to Christ, the head of the body. For we are joined together in his body by his strong sinews, and we grow only as we get our nourishment and strength from God.[169]

Behaviour that promotes and is characterized by condemnation of each other reveals that there are members who are not connected to the head, since they are acting in a way that is completely unlike the head. John, in chapter 1 of his gospel, describes Jesus as having come in "grace and truth";[170] there was never a hint of condemnation on Jesus' part as he spoke with others regarding the Good News. The community Paul describes in Ephesians is one in which everyone exercises their gift under the direction of Christ the head and in support of the community as a whole – and the only environment that fosters this kind of collaborative participation is love. As God's people interact with each other and with others outside the community, they behave with grace and truth – like Jesus, the head to which they are connected and from which they take their direction. John the Apostle makes this relation quite explicit in his first letter to the believing community:

---

[168] Romans 12:9 (NLT).

[169] Col 2:16–19 (NLT).

[170] In that order, as is demonstrated throughout John's gospel in Jesus' encounters with people such as the man at the pool of Bethsaida and the Samaritan woman at the well. I owe this insight to Rikk Watts, Professor of New Testament at Regent College, Vancouver, British Columbia.

Dear friends, let us continue to love one another, for love comes from God. Anyone who loves is born of God and knows God. But anyone who does not love does not know God – for God is love. God showed how much he loved us by sending his only Son into the world so that we might have eternal life through him. This is real love. It is not that we loved God, but that he loved us and sent us his Son as a sacrifice to take away our sins. Since God loved us that much, we surely ought to love each other.[171]

We see that in this section of the letter Paul has presented his readers with a great challenge: to work toward becoming the community that God desires. He wants the readers to take hold of what God has given by His Spirit so that they will always be focused on Christ, trusting God and living out their faith in an environment of love. He is looking for maturity from both leaders and members as they work together to live out their new humanity in the world. Reading and following these same encouragements many centuries later, we continue to be molded and shaped into God's people; so much time has passed since Paul wrote these words, and we are still working toward becoming God's community! The ideal is always before us as we look to what we will become in Christ at the end. In the meantime there is community to be had in the present that can change the world by demonstrating the fulfillment of God's plan to restore humanity. Evil can be pushed back; good can prevail.

That is the community Paul describes and encourages through the words he has written so far. The next section of the letter will push the believers ever further and deeper in their understanding of their new life in Christ, so that there will be no doubt what God's community is to look like as it lives focused on Christ, under His direction, and in loving relationships that show forth the love of the Father, Son, and Spirit for each other and for us.

---

[171] 1 John 4:7–11 (NLT).

Chapter Seven

LIVING AS CHILDREN OF LIGHT

Ephesians 4:17–24

*I say this to you on behalf of the Lord: don't live anymore the way others[172]
do. They live out of the emptiness of their mind. The lights aren't on inside.[173]
They live far away from God because they don't know him on the inside and
the emptiness has hardened their hearts. Because of this, they have developed
a stomach[174] for dirty deeds and their lust is insatiable. But you didn't come
to know of Christ in this way, if you really did hear of him and were taught
the truth about him. What you learned was to put away your old way of
living, which only made you worse because of the insatiable appetite for
empty things, and to be renewed in the spirit of your mind. Put on your new
humanity that has been created for righteous relationship and holy living.*

RENEWAL OF THE MIND

Paul now delves even deeper into distinguishing between being part of God's
community and being distant or alienated from God's community. There is
an affinity here with what he shares at the beginning of chapter 2 of the letter,
about "walking dead people" who "follow carnal desires". Those that are alienated
from God live a life where the "lights aren't on!" They walk in the darkness,
groping for what will satisfy the flesh. There is no Spiritual awareness on the
inside; there is nothing but emptiness, which they seek to fill only by satiating

---

[172] Paul's words are literally "like other nations", i.e., the pagans or Gentiles. Since Paul has made
a point of showing that both Jews and Gentiles are included in the new humanity, he cannot be
referring to ethnicity per se here; rather, he is making an analogy between those who don't yet know
Christ and the pagans who (unlike Israel) were ignorant of the true God. He is talking about how
"others" live who do not have the light of Christ.

[173] The actual phrase is εσκοτωμενοι τη διανοια literally meaning "out of the darkness of
their understanding". I wanted to highlight the parallel between this idea and the "zombie-like"
nature of those "who are dead" at the beginning of chapter 2. As he urges his readers to live in
the light of new humanity and not the darkness of depravity, Paul is bringing home to them
the desperate condition of humanity alienated from God. No doubt life in the Empire brought
daily challenges to believers trying to "walk" in the light of the new humanity given by Christ,
and the same is true for us today: darkness is all around, as well as within the believer. Only light
will eliminate it.

[174] Paul uses the word απηλγηκοτες from the root απαλγεω, which carries the meaning of
"becoming callous". See Bauer, *A Greek English Lexicon of the New Testament*, p. 80.

carnal desires. Their lack of awareness of spiritual need leads to an appetite only for the superficial and the carnal.

This is the sinister life of one who is alienated from God. One easily recalls the parable told by Jesus, of the Lost Son who goes off to the far country and spends his inheritance on coarse living. Exhausting all his resources, he winds up empty, both materially and relationally. Reduced to eating the same slop that the pigs are given on the farm where he ends up living, the son remembers images of a better life in the house of his father. He remembers what life should be like, as opposed to the empty life he is now living,[175] and realizes that even his father's servants have it better than he does in his present state of destitution.

In a similar way, Paul is reminding his readers what life was like before they met Christ, when they lived apart from God. This base and pathetic existence is characterized by an insatiable appetite to satisfy the desires of the flesh; the appetite is insatiable because what is consumed only adds to the emptiness and creates a hardening of the heart that sends the individual into deeper and darker places to find satisfaction. Having lost all moral compass, the person in this condition sinks to a depth of depravity whose actions know no boundaries. It is a web woven by evil to trap people, twist their humanity, and render them completely helpless to restore their relationship with God.

Paul makes it clear that followers of Christ did not come to know Him through such an existence. Rather, it was God who revealed Himself to them in Christ, showing them what they could not see on their own: both the cure and the disease. Again, here we have echoes of what Paul shares in the second half of chapter 1 of the letter; the "eyes of their heart"[176] were opened to the reality of Christ and the love of the Father, while the Spirit entered and began the work of healing and restoring their identity in relationship with the Father, Son, and Spirit. This allowed them, in turn, to understand that the old way of living is not true human living at all; there is a new way of living as restored humanity, given by Christ and made active in us by His Spirit. This new way of living comes with a renewal of the mind, so that the mind is oriented toward God and functions out of an understanding of what true humanity should look like and how it is to be lived.

What needs to change is how the mind directs the actions of the body. Without Christ, the mind is darkened and bent by carnal desire; with Christ, on the other hand, the mind is renewed so as to understand what true humanity is when lived in its fullness in connection to the Father, Son, and Spirit. The

---

[175] Luke 15:11–31.

[176] Eph 1:18 – translating the literal "eyes of your heart" with "the eyes of your mind".

phrase Paul uses here is "the spirit of your mind". As in Romans 12:2, where Paul encourages the readers to be "transformed by the renewing of their mind", so here Paul encourages the readers to be renewed "in the spirit of their mind". The phrase "spirit of your mind"[177] is a different way of saying that what is needed is knowledge of the truth, the Good News that is Christ, and this new knowledge needs to form the foundation for one's whole outlook on life and living. Behind both of these phrases is the New Testament concept expressed by the Greek word *metanoia*.[178] Although Paul does not use this word in either passage, he is referencing the same concept, which has to do not only with receiving and accepting correct information – a change in mental furniture, as it were – but more specifically with changing the way we see ourselves and the world around us. The person now has a different outlook and a completely different point of view because of what they now know; their new knowledge, given by God Himself, informs all of their thinking and decision-making, their desires, the way they evaluate and interpret everything. No longer prowling around like a walking dead person, the individual now sees differently due to a change in thinking. This change in thinking is related to an understanding of what Paul has shared in the letter so far: the story of God's connection to and love for creation, and His plan to renew it.

This change of thinking is related also to a change of heart. The heart was hardened from a life of lewd living; but now, after encountering Christ and the story of God's secret plan for renewing the world, the heart has been softened by the work of God's Spirit making known the love of Christ. This love, as we have already seen, is expressed in the adoption of humanity and its full inclusion in the triune relationship of Father, Son, and Spirit. When individuals experience a change in both mind and heart as to who they are in the eyes of the Father who created and redeemed them, and as to their purpose in the world, then life in a community that "builds itself up in love" becomes possible. It is possible through

---

[177] Gordon D. Fee, *God's Empowering Presence: The Holy Spirit in the Letters of Paul* (Peabody, MA: Hendrickson, 1994), pp. 711–712. "…[I]t seems most likely to me that they would have heard this phrase in terms of the Spirit, either directly or indirectly, as lying very close to whatever renewing work takes place in their own spirits. Probably, therefore, this is yet another instance where we should recognize the human spirit as the first referent, but be prepared also to recognize the Holy Spirit as hovering nearby, since in Paul's own theology, such renewal is indeed the work of the Spirit."

[178] *Metanoia* is the Greek for "change of mind". See Colin Brown, ed., *The New International Dictionary of New Testament Theology*, vol. 1, p. 357. On page 358, it is noted that "There are many passages in which the term *metanoeo* does not appear, but in which the thought of repentance is clearly present." This comment is in direct reference to the occurrence of *metanoia* in the gospels, but it is also true of Paul's letters.

connection with Christ, and through the work of the Spirit:[179] drawing on the Spirit's strength gives one the ability to live out of the new humanity described by Paul earlier in chapter 4.[180]

Paul is urging the believers to take full advantage of the change that has already taken place. It sounds as if he realizes that not all of them have fully embraced that change yet; some are still struggling[181] with the old humanity. Recalling for them what they were taught about Christ, Paul urges them to continue "putting off" the old and "putting on" the new. The new humanity they are to "put on" is in full and open relationship with the Father, Son, and Spirit, and is therefore characterized by holy living – that is, living in the love and grace and fellowship that constitute the holiness of God. As Paul described it in chapter 2 of the letter, the new humanity obtained by Christ has unobstructed access to God and lives in peace and harmony both with God and with others. Those who participate in it through Christ are bonded together into a new community in which God's Spirit dwells. This type of living isn't just about "keeping one's nose clean";[182] it's about living out the image of God in us, living as God's "work of art"[183] – His true masterpieces, engaging the world around us in the fruit of our relationship with God so that the good we live out enhances the world He has created.

It could not have been easy to cast off the old way of living when surrounded by the corrupt and bankrupt culture of the Roman Empire. With the multitude of pagan gods and pagan rituals of worship, as described earlier in this book, came a dehumanization and despair among the masses that left little room even for basic dignity and decency. Leaving the lifestyle perpetuated by this environment would

---

[179] F. F. Bruce, *The Epistles to the Colossians to Philemon and to the Ephesians: The New International Commentary on the New Testament* (Grand Rapids, MI: Eerdmans, 1984), p. 358. "This inward renewal is the work of the Holy Spirit, progressively transforming believers into the image of Christ, 'from one degree of glory to another' (2 Cor. 3:18). It is by the Spirit's power, too, that 'the inner being is being renewed every day,' no matter to what attrition the body may be exposed (2 Cor. 4:16), until what is mortal is 'swallowed up by life' – a consummation of which the Spirit is the present guarantee (2 Cor. 5:4–5)."

[180] N. T. Wright, *Paul for Everyone: Prison Letters* (Louisville, KY: Westminster John Knox Press, 2004) EPub File, p. 159. "Now that they are 'in Christ', they have the responsibility, in the power of the Spirit, to take off the old lifestyle, the old way of being human, like someone stripping of a shabby and worn suit of clothing. It may have become comfortable. You may be used to it, and even quite like it. Familiar clothes are often like that, and brand new ones often feel a bit strange. But if you want to live as a new person in and for the king, the old suit of clothes has to come off, and the new one has to go on."

[181] Cf. Eph 4:2.

[182] In other words, it isn't about keeping up a perfect moral performance – it is much deeper than that.

[183] Cf. Eph 2:10.

be a process in which each individual would need to "put off" and "put on" on a daily basis. The emphasis of Paul on their "walk" intimates the ongoing, daily need to reorient one's mind and heart toward Christ and let the Spirit continue the work of renewing from the inside out. Living in community together was not only part of the goal; it was crucial to reaching the goal, because it was part of the Spirit's way of sustaining the process of renewal.

It is clear that the way to keep "putting off" the old humanity and "putting on" the new is to continue in a fully engaged relationship with Christ. In his book *After We Believe*, N. T. Wright makes an excellent plea for believers to gain ground in the virtues that keep them close to Christ and in the new humanity. This doesn't just happen by chance, nor is it "caught" in one random encounter. It is developed by engaging continually in relationship with Christ, "dwelling" in it, so that one breathes holy living as His follower. It demands work.[184] It requires that we continually give ourselves to be trained and formed by God's Spirit in the character of the image of God. Otherwise we run the risk of failing to react, in moments of crisis, in a way that will bring good to others and to the creation around us. Wright explains that this discipline is something that can only be achieved over time as believers stay committed to Christ and submissive to the Spirit as the constant source that forms their character into what God desires. This focus on our formation and training as people of God's community allows us to mature to the point where behaviour in keeping with the character of God becomes "second nature" or habitual.

Paul is emphasizing such formation to his readers as he builds toward a description of the ultimate goal of God's community in His secret plan for renewing the world. In chapter 6 of the letter, he will show them that they have the privilege of joining God, at His invitation, in the battle against evil. Part of God's plan for renewal is the presence of His community on earth, in this age before Christ returns, to join Him in pushing back evil by doing good – a theme that Paul has woven throughout the letter so far.[185] Until such time as the Lord Jesus finally comes and purges the world of all evil, God's community

---

[184] N. T. Wright, *After You Believe: Why Christian Character Matters* (San Francisco: HarperCollins e-books; EPub file), chapter 5: "Transformed by the Renewal of Your Mind", pp. 10–11. "For Paul, faith, hope, and love are already given in Christ and by the Spirit, and it is possible to live by them. But you have to work at it. And to work at it you have to want to live in the daytime. You have to understand how your own moral life functions. You have to think through what it all means and how it all works. You have to develop, consciously and deliberately, the habits of heart, mind, soul, and strength that will sustain this life of faith, hope, and love."

[185] See for example 2:10, as well as chapter 4 about the nature of "giving" that characterizes the community as an influence of good on the world around it.

exists to be the "leavening" or "salting" influence so that evil is driven back and good prevails. This is only possible if believers live out their new humanity in relationship with Father, Son, and Spirit and so create the habits and character that enable them to respond as Christ does.

In the next passage, Paul will go into more detail, addressing daily speech and conversation and other behaviour to make sure that it evidences the new humanity.

Ephesians 4:25–5:2

So put off lying; everyone speak the truth with their neighbour because we belong to each other. Get angry, but don't sin: don't let the sun go down on your anger and don't give any room for the devil. The thief will steal no more. The worker will work with his hands for good in order to give to the one who has need. Let no bad words come out of your mouth. Use words that are good for building up the one who needs it, so that it benefits[186] the one who hears. Don't sadden the Holy Spirit who has sealed you for the day of redemption. Put off all bitterness, fierceness, shouting, and slander, along with all wickedness. Be kind to one another, sympathetic, forgiving each other, just as God in Christ forgave you.

Therefore be imitators of God, as children who are loved [by their Father]. Live in love just as Christ loved you and gave Himself for us like the sweet-smelling aroma of an offering and a sacrifice to God.

RENEWAL OF WORDS AND DEEDS

Paul now goes into detail about what "putting off" the old humanity looks like among the people of God's community. He follows a pattern of first identifying what is to be "put off", followed by what to "put on." His starting point for this is our speech, the way we use words; specifically, the issue of lying words. Lying is a most destructive behaviour in a community. It is the earliest form of deception found in the biblical story: the evil one, whom Paul will later call the devil, lied about the character of God to the man and woman in the garden.[187] Lying

---

[186] Frank E. Gaebelein, ed., *The Expositor's Bible Commentary*, vol. 11: *Ephesians through Philemon* (Grand Rapids: Zondervan, 1978), p. 65. Commentator A. Skevington Wood observes, in his commentary on this passage: "'That it may benefit' (*hina do charin*) simply means to confer a blessing, whether temporal or spiritual. The ultimate source of all blessing is God. The channel may be human and so even the everyday conversation of Christians may become a means of grace to others."

[187] More precisely, the serpent raised doubt in the mind of Adam and Eve as to whether God had told them the truth.

destroys trust and leads to the severance of relationship, and is to be avoided at all costs in God's community.

What replaces lying (that is, what we are to "put on") is speaking the truth, and the place to put this into practice is with one's neighbour. Out of several words that can be used for "neighbour"[188], Paul chooses the same one that was used by Jesus when he was asked to identify the greatest commandment. Jesus' reply was twofold: "You must love the Lord your God with all your heart, all your soul, and all your mind," and "Love your neighbour as yourself."[189] Given that Paul has so far focused on how God's people should live out their new humanity with "one another",[190] that is, in mutuality within God's community, his switch to the term "neighbour" is significant. It suggests that this behaviour should be practised not only toward one another in the believing community, but also to anyone who could fall into the category of neighbor, including those not yet part of the community. It should evoke for his readers the teaching of Jesus about who our neighbour is: in Luke 10:29, Jesus answers the question, "Who is my neighbour?" with the parable of the Good Samaritan, illustrating that anyone within proximity at any given moment is our neighbour, regardless of race, ethnicity, gender, colour, or religious belief.[191] Truthtelling is an inherent feature of the new humanity, and therefore is practised with everyone, whether they are in the believing community or in the world at large.

It is interesting that Paul follows this imperative with the proviso that one can "get angry" as long as the anger does not lead to sin. Jumping ahead to 5:1, Paul's encouragement to be "imitators of God" would include the possibility of being appropriately angry, since it is clear from Scripture that God does get angry.[192] Jesus also demonstrates anger, not only in the well-known scene in which He overturns the tables of the moneychangers in the temple, but also in some of

---

[188] The most common word is περιοικεω, περιοικος from the root οικεω, meaning "to house" and therefore with the suffix περι attached meaning "housed next to". φιλος is specifically used for "friend" and is sometimes translated as "neighbour", but more often is paired with γειτων as in Luke 15:6 and 15:9. The word Paul uses here is πλησιον, which is used in Matthew in the teaching of the Beatitudes (Matt. 5:43) and in Jesus' response when questioned about the greatest commandment (Matt. 22:39 as well as in parallel passage in Mark 12:31). Paul uses the same phrase, "love your neighbour as yourself", in Romans 13:9 and Galatians 5:14.

[189] Matthew 22:37–39 (NLT).

[190] αλληλων, appearing in 4:25 as well as 4:2; Paul also uses it twice in verse 32.

[191] I suspect some may find it farfetched to suggest that Paul is alluding to this parable, but given that Paul's crowd heard the letters read out loud, it is in fact quite likely that his use of πλησιον would recall the same word in the story of Jesus and his teaching on the neighbour. It would be a well-told story among believers.

[192] Read through the prophets, such as Ezekiel, and see how God is angered by Israel's disobedience and their following other gods/idols.

His conversations with Jewish religious leaders, on whom He pronounces quite severe "woe" statements.[193] But Paul qualifies "getting angry" with not sinning, which is also in keeping with God's character. God's anger stems from His deep inner love for His creation, and it works toward justice and restoration. God is angered by evil undermining His creation. He gets angry at the destructiveness of idolatry. He gets angry at nations that oppress other nations, or societies in which the rich and powerful oppress the poor and powerless. But God's anger does not end in destruction; rather, it works toward renewal and redemption. Getting angry without sinning, then, is not simply flying off the handle because things are not going our way. The anger Paul speaks of is directed at evil and pushes us toward renewal and reconciliation. John Stott puts it aptly when he emphasizes that we need more of this kind of anger:

> I go further and say that there is a great need in the contemporary world for more Christian anger. We human beings compromise with sin in a way in which God never does. In the face of blatant evil we should be indignant not tolerant, angry not apathetic. If God hates sin, his people should hate it too. If evil arouses his anger, it should arouse ours also. It is particularly noteworthy that the apostle introduces this reference to anger in a letter devoted to God's new society of love, and in a paragraph concerned with harmonious relationships. He does so because true peace is not identical with appeasement.[194]

True peace, as Stott points out, is dependent on members of a community living in humility and kindness, putting up with one another, but never compromising the truth or giving evil a foothold in order to do so. The truth should be addressed quickly and swiftly with all the love that the Spirit has to give us in Christ, so that any fracture that potentially threatens relationships can be eliminated. This is why Paul qualifies "getting angry" with not sinning, and with not letting the sun go down on such anger. Anger that is left to brew will boil over. Better to get it out in the open with love so as to deal with it.

Paul adds one last qualifier: "Don't give any room for the devil." The devil readily takes advantage of anger that turns ugly within God's community, or in

---

[193] Matthew 23:15: "Yes, how terrible it will be for you teachers of religious law and you Pharisees. For you cross land and sea to make one convert, and then you turn him into twice the son of hell that you yourselves are!" says Jesus (NLT). I have no difficulty picturing Jesus angry while saying this to the religious leaders.

[194] John Stott, *The Bible Speaks Today: The Message of Ephesians*, p. 186.

any community; he can smell it a mile away and is attracted by it. He stands at the door of our hearts, but rather than knock to be let in like Christ, he sneaks in without our noticing and turns the anger into the things Paul mentions in verse 31: "bitterness, fierceness, shouting, slander, and all kinds of wickedness". He tries to keep hostility alive in the human race – the very hostility that Jesus put to death in His own Person in order to free us from it. Paul understood all too well how the devil gets a foothold in God's community, and was able to see evil at work and fight against it rather than against people. It was Christ within him, working by His Spirit, that allowed Paul to identify the real enemy. We should do the same, for this reflects the character of God, who has always directed his resistance against evil and the evil one, not against humanity or the creation. Humanity and creation He will renew; evil He will destroy.

In Paul's next words, about stealing, I find an interesting double ring. The obvious sense is that Paul is urging any thieves in the believing community to stop stealing. But there is another possible sense implicit in these words, following as they do on the heels of Paul's remark about not giving room to the devil, that relates to the devil himself – the original thief, who has robbed humanity of its true character and its joyful relationships. I see here a declaration by Paul that the ultimate thief, the devil, will steal no more; the raping and pillaging of God's people is over. Jesus took care of that on the cross and through His sacrifice and resurrection. Rather than behave as the devil does, and so perpetuate his ravages on humanity, we are to go about working productively with our hands so that we can bring good instead of harm and loss to those around us. What is intended here by Paul is more than just benevolence, as important as that is. It is also an intentional working out of our new humanity, so that we thwart evil and bring about the good that occurs when the true humanity is lived out in its fullness in the creation.[195] Jesus gave us a glimpse of such humanity in his incarnational life on earth. Now such behaviour and character is being called for in God's community.

Paul then continues with further instruction on how believers should conduct themselves. God's community, where each lives for the other and all live for God, should be a place where words are used to build up. This is the very nature of love in a community. Words are not used to tear down or to hurt. I love the practicality and simple directness of Paul here: "Don't let any bad words come out of your mouth!" In an age of continuing moral decay, the use of "bad words" – that is, destructive, humiliating, hateful, or misleading speech

---

[195] Again, there are echoes here of Eph 2:10.

– proliferates. This is true in our own culture as it was in the Roman Empire. What is the toll such language takes on a people or community? I believe the ultimate effect remains to be seen in terms of the degradation and demeaning of others, whether it is done out of a perverse attempt at humour or out of intended malice. When left unchecked, such bad language easily becomes embedded in the fabric of a culture or society. Jeffrey A. Winters, in his description of Roman society, writes about the demeaning tone taken toward slaves,[196] and how deeply ingrained it was in the language.

How much better it is to use words that build up! In a community characterized by "building itself up through love", the words that are shared bring a benefit to whoever needs it. Our speech should mirror the kind of love and affirmation displayed by God in the story of the baptism of Jesus, where the voice of the Father in heaven pronounced His great pleasure over His Son. In a world that has virtually no vocabulary to describe such love, God raises up His community to live in an environment of acceptance and embrace, where words are used to communicate love and significance to those who belong.

To do otherwise is to "sadden the Holy Spirit": Paul states that deep sorrow comes over the Spirit when God's community behaves in a way that demeans and destroys others, since it is the very antithesis of the relationship that characterizes the triune community of Father, Son, and Spirit. Jesus did not sacrifice His life and give Himself so that we would continue to live in broken communities, void of relationship and dignity and blind to our true identity as beloved children. I cannot put it any better than C. Baxter Kruger in his book *The Great Dance: The Christian Vision Revisited*:

> Christian faith is first and foremost the discovery of what the Father, Son and Spirit have made of the human race in Jesus Christ. Faith is the discovery that there and then in Jesus Christ we were reconciled, saved, adopted; there and then in Jesus Christ we were cleansed and born again, recreated and taken home to the Father; and there and then in Jesus Christ we were welcomed by God the Father almighty, embraced, accepted, included in the circle of life. Christian faith is first and foremost a discovery of truth in Jesus, the truth about God and the truth about ourselves, the truth of our identity, of who we are, a

---

[196] Jeffrey A. Winters, *Oligarchy* (Cambridge University Press; EPub file), p. 107. Among other things, Winters uses the example of the title *instrumentum vocale*, a term for slaves that put them in a category only slightly higher than *instrumentum semi-vocale*, or "beast of burden", and only two categories away from *instrumentum mutum*, the term for a "blunt object or tool".

discovery of the fact that the Father, Son and Spirit do not live out their dance of life without us. And that is a discovery that commands us to believe it as truth and to rethink everything we thought we knew about ourselves and others and our lives and theirs. That is a discovery that commands us to live in the dignity and joy and freedom of the truth and to recognize no one according to the flesh, as Paul put it, as a 'mere human' [2 Cor 5:16].[197]

The Spirit is the one who seals[198] the community for what God has intended for it, ensuring that the relationship the Father has extended to us through Christ will continue through to the end when we are fully renewed in God's Kingdom established on earth. As in chapter 1 of the letter, Paul here indicates that the Spirit's presence is the guarantee that what God has accomplished in Christ – that is, our redemption and renewal as His new humanity – is and will be effective.[199] Because of this certainty, in a very real sense we already are what we will become, and can therefore conduct our relationships with one another and with those outside the community in a way that reflects what we will become in the end. There is also a very real sense that we have not yet arrived; but the appropriate response to this is not to shrug our shoulders and say, "Oh well, I guess we'll have to wait for the good stuff until the end." Rather, we have access *now* to the goodness of living in God's community – which, though not perfect or complete, is still able by the Spirit to live as God desires, and is attempting to do so on a daily basis. Surely, given the choice, one would prefer to struggle to live in loving community rather than resign oneself to living in an environment where people simply look out for themselves and seek to fulfill their own carnal desires regardless of the impact on anyone else.

Paul then finishes off this section by enumerating the remaining things to "put off." These have already been identified as the kinds of things that occur when anger gets out of control and love is not the focus. "Bitterness, fierceness, shouting, and slander" are characteristic of people fighting with each other in heated argument. They are the typical vehicle of accusation, and promote

---

[197] Baxter Kruger, *The Great Dance: The Christian Vision Revisited* (Vancouver: Regent College, 2005), p. 64–65.

[198] N. T. Wright, *Paul for Everyone: Prison Letters*, p. 188. "The word Paul uses could refer to the 'seal' or official stamp on a document or package, marking it out for a particular use or occasion. The mark indicates who it belongs to and what it's for."

[199] Eph 1:14: "Believing in the truth of such good news of our salvation, the Holy Spirit has sealed this promise to us, He being the guarantee of our inheritance until it comes to be vested fully in us."

strife and alienation in a community. Paul is calling on his readers to have none of it. In the inevitable moments of conflict, they are to react out of love and forgiveness in keeping with the character that is continually being formed in them by the Spirit: Paul asks them to "put on" kindness and to be sympathetic toward each other, quick to offer the kind of forgiveness that they themselves have received from Christ. Anger and other emotional responses will surface, but how the community responds to them will determine how they then continue in relationship. There is nothing more successful in defusing a potentially volatile situation then a kind, calm, gentle approach that communicates a sympathetic, forgiving, Christlike response.

Finally, Paul issues a very bold instruction. He calls on the believers to be "imitators of God". The point being made is not to "be God" but rather, as Paul qualifies in the words that follow, to imitate God as children loved by the Father. In other words, just as a child will pick up the habits, character, and even the tone of the parents in whose presence it lives, so Paul is exhorting us, as God's children, to pick up his habits, character, and tone, and to live accordingly. This ought to be only natural for a community that lives in relationship with Father, Son, and Spirit, for as we participate in the life of the Trinity, the character of God will seep into the character of the community. Besides, if humanity was designed from the beginning to bear the image of God, then bearing that image is what it means to be renewed, restored humanity. The image of God, who lives in loving community as Father, Son, and Spirit, is shown forth in the human community whose members live in love with one another.

This, says Paul, is the kind of offering and sacrifice that is pleasing to God. It is interesting that Paul borrows the Old Testament analogy of sacrifice and offering to characterize the kind of behaviour that pleases God. In the story of Israel, pagan worship is always prevalent among the people of the surrounding nations, and Israel repeatedly succumbs to such worship and the detestable practices that accompany it, including human sacrifice to appease the gods. The hope of those who made such sacrifices was to send a pleasing aroma up to the god in order to avert anger or malevolence. But the Hebrew God was no such deity! His desire for sacrifice was so that relationship could be restored with His creation. The kind of aroma that pleases this God, says Paul, is not the smell of death and burning flesh, but the fragrance produced by people living together in harmony and honouring Him by their love for each other.

Paul will now move into his last address about what to "put off" and "put on" as it relates to sexuality. Given the degenerate sexual mores within the Roman

Empire, it is vitally important that God's people be aware of the sexual behaviour appropriate to those who claim to belong to His community.

Ephesians 5:3-10

Fornication and sexual uncleanness or any such greedy practice should not even be known[200] to exist among you, as is suitable for holy ones. Neither should there be filthiness, foolish conversation, or joking around that is inappropriate, but rather a giving attitude. Be it clear that no sexually unclean fornicator or sexually greedy person [with a taking attitude], for whom sex is his idol, has any inheritance in the Kingdom of Christ and of God. Don't be deceived by anyone who speaks out of their emptiness on these things, because this kind of conduct brings God's anger on those who are related to such disobedience. So don't get involved with them. You did roam around in darkness in the past, but now you are in the light because of the Lord, so walk as children of light. The evidence of light is goodness, righteousness, and truth, showing the way to what pleases the Lord.

TAKING VS. GIVING

Sexuality in the Empire was defined by realities that challenged the conventional family unit. There was an array of sexual practice that fell outside the bonds of marriage. Prostitution was a profession that was legalized and restricted,[201] and some prostitution occurred in the context of religious temples and systems that declared sex to be the pinnacle of religious experience.[202] Homosexuality was common and openly expressed in Roman literature and poetry.[203] It was probably more common than it would normally have been, given the practice

---

[200] The verb ονομαζεσθω appears in the passive voice, indicating that the sexual practices are not only not happening in the community, but not being spoken of with regard to activity in their community. Hence my translation, *"not even be known to exist among you"*

[201] Will Durant, *Caesar and Christ: A History of Roman Civilization and of Christianity from Their Beginnings to A.D. 325* (New York: Simon & Schuster, 1972), p. 369: "The profession was legalized and restricted; brothels (*lupanaria*) were by law kept outside the city walls and could open only at night; prostitutes (*meretrices*) were registered by the aediles and were required to wear the toga instead of the stola. Fees were adjusted to bring promiscuity within the reach of every pocketbook;…"

[202] N. T. Wright, *Paul for Everyone: The Prison Letters*, p. 175. "Some religions, particularly some of those with secret initiation ceremonies, included sexual practices among their rituals. At one end of the scale, this amounted to little more than prostitution with vaguely religious flavour. At the other, it might be suggested that sexual experience was part of the very summit of the religious quest."

[203] Will Durant, *Caesar and Christ*, p. 369. Durant gives evidence of pederasty in the writings of contemporary Roman poets.

of exposing unwanted female babies; this unfortunate form of birth control, along with others that regularly resulted in the death of women, made for an unnaturally low female population in the Empire.[204] A proliferation of unnatural sexual relationships ensued.

It's no wonder Paul refers to inappropriate sexual activity as *porneia*. This word is a catch-all for every inappropriate sexual practice outside of marriage,[205] and every one of them could be readily found in the Rome of Paul's day. This meant that many first-generation believers would have left such lifestyles to join God's community. In fact, the care and stringency with which Paul instructs the believers regarding unacceptable sexual practice in God's community suggests that some of his readers were still struggling with their view of sexuality. He needed to be clear about the kind of sexual behaviour appropriate for those marked out as "holy ones".

Paul is clear in verse 3 that there should be no mention whatsoever of any sexually inappropriate behaviour within God's community. He identifies such inappropriate sexuality as a form of greed, a posture of taking another person for one's own consumption and gratification, that is not only a gross distortion of God's intent for sex but defies the very essence of what it means to be the new human living in God's community. Such behaviour is typical of the "old humanity" that has a voracious appetite for carnal gratification and is never satisfied. It is, as Paul's next injunction shows, accompanied by a way of speaking and thinking about others that regards them as objects to be taken and used without any basis of relationship whatsoever. Whether as an expression of humour or greed, the language that sexually objectifies others is destructive and is to be avoided. What should take its place is a thankful, "giving attitude" that issues in respectful speech. I translated this phrase in this manner to highlight the contrast Paul draws in this passage between "taking" and "giving". A thankful, giving attitude is the product of living in relationship to God. When one lives in Christ, in loving devotion and relationship to Father, Son, and Spirit, one's attitude toward others is giving rather than taking, because that is what the triune God is like. The kind of giving referred to in this context is speech and action that affirms and enhances the humanity of others and causes it to thrive. Living

---

[204] Rodney Stark, *The Rise of Christianity*, p. 122. "…[M]any pagan women still in their childbearing years had been rendered infertile by damage to their reproductive systems from abortions or from contraceptive devices and medicines. In this manner was the decline of the Roman Empire's population ensured."

[205] Colin Brown, *The New International Dictionary of New Testament Theology*, vol. 1, p. 500. "In the Pauline Writings the word-group *porne* denotes any kind of illegitimate sexual intercourse."

in Christ and out of His character, we share with others the renewed humanity He has given us, so that they can in turn live in the new humanity.

Our Western culture has become one characterized by "taking". The highly sexualized language of everyday conversation has objectified the most intimate relationship and experience between a man and a woman. What is deemed to be private and sacred between a husband and a wife has now become exposed to public humiliation, dirty, the butt of jokes, and the expletive of anger. People in our culture go out and get what they need sexually, devoid of love or relationship; sexuality has been reduced to an act. The suffering that this view incurs for both women and men has led to a confused, broken, and abused humanity. This is not the picture of loving community, but rather of walking dead people who have only darkness inside.

Like the culture of the Roman Empire in the 1st century, our own culture has become highly sexualized and relationally bankrupt. Some of this is disguised as "openness" to sexuality, correcting the practice of years gone by where a "closed" view was perpetuated. Certainly the distorted sense of secrecy and shame attached to sexuality in western culture of the 19th century is not to be wished back, but the pendulum swing to the other extreme, to complete lack of restraint and the public exposure of all things sexual in the 20th and 21st centuries, has created another distortion. God has created us as sexual beings, and sex was given as a gift of intimacy, but it is destructive to pretend that every kind of sexual expression is equally appropriate and honouring to that gift.[206] Anyone who lives in this way, writes Paul, has no part in the Kingdom of God; the sexual degradation of *porneia* has a spiritual hold on such an individual that cuts him or her off from life in Christ.[207] Given this potential, it is important that Paul communicate clearly about the boundaries of sexuality.

Paul mentions that there are those who have a lot to say about sexuality but speak from the emptiness inside them. There were all kinds of individuals in that context, as there are in our own, who are ready to explain why certain sexual behaviours are permissible or beneficial, but they do so in a way that distorts the very foundation established by God. Later in chapter 5, Paul will identify the foundational relationship between the sexes as that of husband and wife: the love shared between the two is a reflection of the commitment and love that Christ

---

[206] N. T. Wright, *Paul for Everyone: Prison Letters*, p. 174. "In that world, as in ours, many people saw no need for restraint. If it seemed fun at the time, why not go ahead?"

[207] Colin Brown, *The New International Dictionary of New Testament Theology*, vol. 1, p. 500–501. "it is ...as if a religious and demonic power is let loose in *porneia*. 'It is manifestly a different spirit, a *pneuma akatharton* (Matt. 10:1), a spirit that is incompatible and irreconcilable with Christ, which takes control of man in *porneia.*'" Brown is quoting Hans Iwand.

has for God's community.[208] This is the context for which sex was created, and anything else will be a cheap imitation that twists the intimacy accompanying sex and replaces giving with taking. Only those who are empty inside can accept activity that is not in keeping with what God created as wholesome and intimate in marriage; Paul warns his readers not to listen to them or to become involved with them.[209]

The problem of permissive sexual behaviour was particularly rampant in Corinth, as evidenced by the communication Paul had with the Corinthian churches on this topic. Paul's response in chapter 6 of 1Corinthians to a slogan existing in that community, "I am allowed to do anything," was "Not everything is good for you."[210] It was in the name of "knowledge" and "wisdom" that the Corinthians were engaging in this behaviour, but they were betraying ignorance and lack of wisdom in that they were failing to observe the ironic reality that permissiveness leads to slavery. This is what Paul is warning the Corinthians about when he says, "Even though 'I am allowed to do anything,' I must not become a slave to anything."[211] Slavery is the inevitable outcome when people give themselves over to such sexual permissiveness.

As God's community, we stand to take up an important role in speaking out in favour of the proper relational context for sexuality. We need also to speak out against the inappropriate sexual behaviour that destroys families and individuals. We need to be as vocal as we can to resist the call to empty permissiveness. Above all, we must take our advice from God on this issue, not from so-called experts uninformed by biblical principles, so that there is absolutely no confusion in our faith communities about what sexuality should look like for those living in the new humanity.

Sexuality is very fundamental to our humanity, and sexual behaviour affects the core of our being in a deep and lasting way that often seeps into other areas of life. It is not surprising, then, that Paul indicates God's anger is directed toward those who engage in *porneia* and who speak out of the emptiness of their behaviour; God becomes angry at anything that will undermine His creation. A distorted view of sexuality and immoral sexual practice is very destructive, and will bear God's judgment; He will not put up with it for long. If you want to get into the path of an angry father, just go after his children. You will see a loving,

---

[208] Eph 5:21–25.
[209] Frank E. Gaebelein, ed., *The Expositor's Bible Commentary*, vol. 11, p. 69. Skevington Wood puts it appropriately that "[Paul's] indictment includes all the propagandists of permissiveness."
[210] 1 Cor 6:12 (NLT).
[211] Ibid.

tender father lash out in a way that sends the message, "My kids are not to be touched!" Such is the nature of our loving Father, the Father of our Lord Jesus Christ.

Paul ends this section by reminding the believers that some of them did previously live in darkness. He uses the word "roam" to describe their past lifestyle, evoking the image of roaming about in the darkness looking for the next fix that will satisfy carnal desires. There is no doubt that God had mercy on them; His anger, after all, is ultimately redemptive. Grace is available to those living in the darkness, but they often can't see it. But Paul's readers have seen the light, "because of the Lord," and are now living in it. Light enables God's community to discern what pleases God. Evidence of living in the light is the presence of goodness, righteousness, and truth. This mention of "what pleases the Lord" is a follow-up to the statement in 5:2 concerning the sacrifice and offering that produces a sweet aroma for God. When people live in the new humanity as God's community, it gives God deep pleasure. It has been His desire from the beginning that we live as His unified family in the fullness of the humanity He gave us. God takes joy over a husband and wife loving each other and finding their sexual fulfillment in giving themselves to each other. Anything less falls short of the new humanity that Christ has recovered for us.

Our culture has created a conundrum. The media seeks to prolong adolescence in young adults, and our culture encourages them to delay marriage, while at the same time pushing them to engage in sex earlier and earlier. Lack of maturity combined with premature exposure to and experimentation with sexuality leads to promiscuity. And sadly, God's community today is assuming the same environment for its young people. We are not taking up the responsibility to teach them a biblical view of sexuality, so our young adults are left to try and make sense of this very complex issue all by themselves.[212] Most of the time, they absorb the view presented in the media and succumb to the outlets provided by our culture to satisfy their sexual needs. What we should be doing is introducing young people to the beauty and delight of sexual intimacy within the context of marriage, and helping them work toward making earlier commitments to a life partner so they can enjoy that intimacy appropriately. Rather than prolonging their adolescence, we should be shortening it to its proper length, nudging them toward responsibility, and instilling a mature outlook on life in general. This means speaking to them about marriage earlier than we do. A walk through the

---

[212] Having spent many years in ministry to young adults, I have found that we have not taken up the responsibility to prepare them with a biblical view of sexuality. We have let the media define their sexuality.

Song of Solomon shows the awareness, in Hebrew culture, of how important it is to share with their young people the value of intimacy in marriage, so that they "awaken love when it is time."[213] After marriage, we should follow them and mentor them into becoming mature married couples who learn how to foster intimacy and friendship over time, so that the older they get the more love they share. This is in keeping with a loving community that cares for each other and promotes the new humanity.

Ephesians 5:11–14

Don't engage in the worthless acts of darkness, but rather expose them.[214] It is shameful even to talk about what goes on in secret. But everything exposed by the light is seen for what it truly is,[215] for all that is made visible is light. Take to heart the saying:

"Wake up sleeper, rise from the dead, and Christ will shine on you."

EXPOSING THE DARKNESS

Paul now gives advice about the proper response of God's community as it encounters darkness. In a way that seems to foreshadow the chapter 6 call to join God in battling against evil, the measures Paul commends now move from strictly defensive to more offensive. Where previously he advised his readers to avoid listening to those that promote permissiveness, and to keep away from them, here he addresses the "acts" or "works" of darkness and recommends exposing them. Paul believes there are forces at work that deceive people into engaging in immorality by misrepresenting evil as good. Exposing the evil and bringing it into the light shows those who are held in its grasp how truly evil it is. The goal of such exposing activity is not to judge but to redeem; the enemy is darkness and evil, not the people in its grip. As the light has shone in the hearts of the readers, exposing their old humanity and emptiness so that they turned away from it and embraced the humanity Christ gives, so it can shine in the lives of "others",[216] exposing evil for what it is and waking them up to

---

[213] Song of Solomon 8:4 (NLT): "I want you to promise, O women of Jerusalem, not to awaken love until the time is right."

[214] Frank E. Gaebelein, ed., *The Expositor's Bible Commentary*, vol. 11, p. 70. "When the object is a person, the verb (*elegcho*) means to convince or reprove. This is the distinctive work of the Spirit. But when the object is impersonal, *elegcho* may signify to bring to light or expose."

[215] Paul uses the word φανερουται which means "to be visible." I have taken the opportunity to contextualize the comment based on what Paul is writing so that the intent is clear. Light makes darkness out for what it truly is so that there is no question as to its reality in a person's life.

[216] Cf. Eph 4:17

the reality offered by Christ, so that they allow Him to enter and give them His new humanity.

There is no point, as God's community, in mulling over evil and classifying it, discussing its various nuances, degrees, and categories. Sometimes we waste a lot of time and effort doing this, but Paul makes it clear that there is no point even talking about what goes on in the darkness; the appropriate response to it is exposure. But this exposure is not to be carried out in a way that destroys the individual in the darkness. One need only look at Jesus, and how He engaged sinners such as prostitutes and tax collectors, to see how He entered into the life of the individual and communicated His love and peace while letting them know that He knew their reality, in this way helping them to face the true nature of their situation. A case in point is the woman at the well in John 4. Demonstrating the fullness of "grace and truth" in which He has come, as described by John in his prologue, Jesus shows the Samaritan woman grace, and then lets her know that he knows the truth about her darkness: grace first, which opens the way for truth. His response to her then is to offer her eternal life.[217] As His community, His body, we also can engage those in the darkness with grace and truth. Knowing the individual's darkness, and letting them know we know, is a way of exposing it. But this truth must be offered from within a relationship of grace, conveying love and respect for the person's dignity. Offering the light of Christ, we can be vehicles of redemption for God in the life of others.

Only exposure to the light of Christ can dispel the evil darkness that covers the eyes of those in the old humanity. Paul writes that light makes everything visible. In fact, his brief words at the beginning of verse 14 make it somewhat difficult to know just what he is referring to, though the context of the passage helps us make an educated guess at a couple of options. The first has to do with the simple yet odd-sounding statement that "everything made visible is light". If this is exactly what Paul intended, then he is perhaps referring to the fact that God's community, by living in the light, makes visible a unity and love whose contrast with evil becomes evident to those who have had their dark deeds exposed; it attractively fills their field of vision, and transforms them. Once the light has come, darkness cannot exist.[218] The second interpretive option is that

---

[217] Jesus says in John 4:10, "If you only knew the gift God has for you and who I am, you would ask me, and I would give you living water" – "the water I give …takes away thirst altogether. It becomes a perpetual spring within them, giving them eternal life" (NLT).

[218] John Stott, *The Bible Speaks Today: The Message of Ephesians*, p. 200: "But he [Paul] seems to be describing a second stage in what light does; it actually *transforms what it illumines into light* [my emphasis]. This may mean that Christians who lead a righteous life thereby restrain and reform evildoers, yes, and even convert them."

Paul is simply emphasizing the previous verse, and meant to say "everything is clear (made visible) in the light". This too can have an evangelistic sense, meaning that God's community, by bringing the light of Christ, makes all things clear as to what is (and is not) in keeping with the new humanity. Either way, I think this statement identifies the impact that God's community can have on those in the darkness when it lives in the light of Christ.

What follows appears to be a quotation of, or an allusion to, a combination of Old Testament Scriptures. This is a device used elsewhere in the New Testament as well.[219] Many scholars believe that Paul is quoting part of the liturgy that accompanied a believer's baptism – that the original compilation from which the line is drawn was a first-century hymn sung at the baptismal service of believers, addressing what has occurred in their life upon their conversion.[220] They have awakened from their roaming throughout the darkness in their old humanity and have had the light of Christ shine on them with the new humanity. These words would remind readers of many baptismal celebrations where they had heard the conversion story of fellow believers and seen their public declaration of Christ's work in their life. This awakening can become reality for anyone roaming the darkness; as God's community, there is the opportunity to engage those in darkness, expose evil at work in their lives, and shine the light of Christ in their hearts. A sleeping person is not aware of reality, but a person who is awake can recognize what is real; awakened by the light of Christ, those who were in darkness and oblivious to the truth reach out to Him for true life.

It is wonderful to see the potential that God's community has in being the light of Christ and of the new humanity in the world. Likewise, it is discouraging to know that many of us are so caught up in other things that we miss this opportunity. We have been given by God the ability to introduce others to Christ so that they may come to know the marvellous gift of their restored humanity, lived in relationship to the Father, Son, and Spirit. Lack

---

[219] Robert H. Gundry, *Commentary on Ephesians* (Baker Academic, 2010; EPub file), p. 73. "Paul apparently combines passages such as Isaiah 26:19; 51:17; 52:1; 60:1. (We find composite quotations of the Old Testament elsewhere in the New Testament, too – for example, Mark 1:2–3 and Matthew 27:9–10.)"

[220] William Hendriksen, *New Testament Commentary: Galatians and Ephesians* (Grand Rapids, MI: Baker, 1989), pp. 235–236. "It is conceivable that though Eph 5:14 is in the final analysis rooted in Isa. 60:1, the form in which the latter passage is here reproduced by Paul was that of lines from an early Christian hymn. The hymn, in other words, may have been based on the Isaiah passage. It is clear at any rate that when Paul was writing what is now called the fifth chapter of Ephesians he had hymns in mind, for he mentions them only a few verses later, namely, in 5:19."

of unity, an unwillingness to honour God-given diversity, taking our focus off Christ, distortion of our God-given sexuality, and having a taking rather than a giving attitude all contribute to our inability to be God's community and so drive back evil with good. Only when we truly get our act together as God's community can we have the life-changing impact on others that Paul is calling the readers of the Ephesian letter to have in this passage. Imagine the broken lives healed and restored by Christ! Imagine the deceived people, groping around in the darkness and abused by one more thing that will not even come close to satisfying their emptiness, freed from the clutches of evil! Imagine the love that can be restored and flourish in a community when those who follow Christ, and are in relationship with the triune God of grace, live out of the abundance of that relationship. It is wonderful enough to sing about and proclaim in a world that so desperately needs it.

Ephesians 5:15–21

Pay attention to being careful not to live unwisely but to be wise, redeeming the time, because we live in evil days. So don't be foolish, but understand what God wants. Don't get drunk on wine; you'll wind up empty. Be filled by the Spirit, [and when you're together] share psalms, hymns, and spiritual songs with each other, singing and making music in your heart to the Lord, giving thanks for everything in the name of our Lord Jesus Christ and to God our Father. Submit to each other out of reverence for Christ.

A COMMUNITY FILLED WITH THE SPIRIT

Given what's at stake in terms of those in darkness finding the light, Paul advises the readers to be careful and circumspect about how they live. Knowing the power of Christ within our community, we should make the most of every moment we have to live according to the new humanity. We are called to be a light shining in the world so as to expose the darkness in the lives of others and make Christ visible to them. We can't be cavalier or foolish about this; we need to keep our heads about us and stay connected as God's community, bringing the fight to evil's doorstep and not to each other. If we behave like the others who walk around in darkness, then we stand to lose ourselves. We also lose our focus and our source of light. If we fail to be who we are called to be, we are then unable to help others.

The reality in Paul's day, and in ours for that matter, is that the days are evil. The Empire was being led by self-imposed oligarchic despots who made a career out of protecting their interests at the cost of others.[221] The society was saturated with relatively poor and powerless people attempting to feed off the rich. The imposition of a structure where a chosen few managed all the land and resources created less than ideal conditions for the rest. In this inequitable environment, God's community was able to make a difference, and crucial to doing so was their wisdom, focus, intentionality, and strategic use of the gifts God had given them to bless others. They reached out to the unwanted and unfortunate in the Empire and literally saved lives by their deep care and concern.[222] At the same time, Christians were subject to persecution; living in such delicate circumstances demanded that they be circumspect in dealing with people and situations. Staying connected as God's community, taking care to act wisely, and living out their common belief in decency and equality for fellow human beings, Christians were able, over time, to expose darkness in the Empire and bring light to its people.

We too need to keep our heads about us. We need to capitalize on our present freedom to live openly as God's community and maintain an environment of love for others. Living out of the abundance of relationship with Father, Son, and Spirit, we can continue to make a huge difference in the lives of others. After all, those first-century Christians carried on a tradition of community that eventually converted an entire Empire.[223] When we live in unity with God and with each other, it is not hard to know His will. We can be in no doubt as to what God wants. What He wants is that others be rescued from the darkness and be adopted into His family, and He wants our participation with Him in bringing this about.

In order to stay true to this calling, it's important that we be indwelt by the Spirit as God's community. The verb "be filled" in this passage is plural; Paul is addressing not just each individual *per se*, but all members of the community

---

[221] Jeffrey A. Winters, *Oligarchy* (Cambridge University Press; EPub file), pp. 105–116. Winters itemizes the make-up of land ownership and income in the Roman Empire. The landowners of the Empire made up three percent of the entire population.

[222] Rodney Stark, *The Rise of Christianity*, chapter x, "Epidemics, Networks and Conversion". Stark indicates that Christians, caring for both their own and for pagans during the plagues that riddled the Empire, were able to decrease the mortality rate in cities where there was a pronounced Christian presence.

[223] Ibid., p. 10. "Looking at the rise of a Christian majority as purely a function of a constant rate of growth calls into serious question the emphasis given by Eusebius and others to the conversion of Constantine as the factor that produced the Christian majority (Grant 1977). So long as nothing changed in the conditions that sustained the 40-percent-a-decade growth rate, Constantine's conversion would better be seen as a response to the massive exponential wave in progress, not as its cause."

together, the group as a whole. We need to let God's Spirit indwell us and our communities so that He can continue to make us into the new humanity God desires.

It is interesting that Paul addresses the issue of drinking here. No doubt drunkenness was prevalent in the Empire. Given all the festivals honouring various pagan gods, there was always an occasion to revel and to let loose. The Romans borrowed this religious revelry from the Greeks; they even had a god in their pantheon whose particular sphere of oversight was strong drink, and they conducted celebrations in his honour with a keen sense of ritual.[224] It was common to head out to the country or the banks of the Tiber and revel in music, drinking, and unrestrained sexual activity.[225] The focus was to celebrate the fruitfulness of the earth and so of life. In this pagan religious context, strong drink was also used to induce a state of ecstasy.[226] Combining drunkenness, sexual immorality, and pagan worship, these ritual festivals were bound to lead participants into the "worthless acts of darkness" about which Paul writes earlier in chapter 5, and so incur God's anger. Paul urges the readers not to get drunk on wine as a way of producing happiness or inducing an ecstatic experience. Since this is a general letter to all churches, it seems that drinking too much wine was common enough among believers for Paul to make a point of it in this letter.[227] Drinking too much wine leads to emptiness. Where other translators use the word "dissipation", I have used "emptiness" in order to make Paul's point more vividly; the Greek word he uses refers to a depleting or wasting of one's resources, both physically and spiritually, until they are completely gone.[228] The way to

---

[224] Ross Shepard Kraemer and Mary Rose D'Angelo, *Women and Christian Origins* (Oxford University Press, 1999; EPub file), p. 14.

[225] Ibid., p. 14.

[226] Kirk Summers, "Lucretius's Roman Cybele," in *Cybele, Attis and Related Cults: Essays in Memory of M. J. Vermaseren*, ed. Maarten Jozef Vermaseren and Eugene Lane (Leiden: E. J. Brill, 1996), p. 356. Summers cites a quote from a contemporary of Cicero describing a dancer performing during a Cybelene worship ceremony, "…who knew how to drink down a cup of strong wine, thrice in a row, here she takes a rest under the elms, no longer delighted by love, no longer by the tiring all-night festivals. A great farewell, revelries and frenzies: she lies buried …who was formerly crowned with a wreath of flowers."

[227] Cf. 1 Cor 11:20–21: "It's not the Lord's Supper you are concerned about when you come together. For I am told that some of you hurry to eat your own meal without sharing with others. As a result, some go hungry while others get drunk" (NLT).

[228] Frank Gaebelein, ed., *The Expositor's Bible Commentary*, vol. 11, p. 72. Commentator Skevington Wood points out that "[t]he danger of drunkenness (Gal 5:21) lies not only in itself but in what it may induce. Debauchery (*asotia*) in the NT means dissoluteness or dissipation. It is the 'wild living' of the prodigal son (Luke 15:13, adverb). In classical Greek it signified extravagant squandering both of money and of the physical appetites. If they are wise, Christians will avoid all such excess."

ruin yourself is to seek a cheap, quick thrill by getting drunk, typically at the cost of imposing on or violating others and in the process reducing both them and yourself to emptiness. Paul warns Christians not to take this route. This is the way that those who live in darkness go about seeking happiness.

If there is a way to make a play on words, Paul does not hesitate to capitalize on it, and this is no exception: rather than be "emptied" by consuming too much wine, he suggests that the readers be "filled" with the Spirit. *Drinking* or *filling up* on wine will lead to *emptiness*; letting God's Spirit *fill us up* will lead to true *fullness*. This fullness creates a deep happiness of being. It is the kind of happiness that exists when God's community is living out the new humanity, which Paul now describes using a string of participles: sharing songs, singing, making music, giving thanks, submitting. Being filled with the Spirit brings the community together to engage in true celebration, with psalms and hymns of praise, songs, poetry, and music that wells up from the heart to express the gratitude and joy that comes from living in a community of love. Singing and giving thanks to God for all that He is and has done is the most natural response. Submitting to each other (v. 21) is also an act of worship, of "reverence to Christ". The sense here is that the environment of love in God's community creates a desire to give to each other in humility, laying down our personal agendas for the sake of one another so that each one's humanity is upheld and affirmed. This honours God because it is the nature of the community in the Trinity. It is complete joy to experience the same Trinitarian culture of fellowship with each other.

Singing, offering, making music, giving thanks, submitting: these are the actions that describe the full experience of the Spirit's indwelling when we live as God's community. The Spirit who changes us from the inside out causes us to experience the breadth and depth of relationship with Christ so that we experience the fullness of life with the Trinity. To top it all off, God will do even more than we can imagine or think because He loves us!

When this is happening in earnest, there is absolutely no substitute. Can you envision what your community could look like if it were living like this? You have to go right back to chapter 4, verse 1 to trace all the characteristics of God's community when it is living in the new humanity. It is what God has intended for us all along, and it can be so if we set our hearts and minds to let the Spirit work within us to create the right kinds of habits in our relationships. If you're wondering what a "Spirit-filled" follower of Christ looks like, then go back through the letter and create a list of characteristics from Paul's instruction so far.

Along with being a community that lives in love, exercises patience one with another, focuses on the Trinitarian God for its unity in diversity, and has its leaders and members all giving and ministering to each other according to their gifts, comes maturity. Maturity enables members to build one another up continually and to avoid being blown away or distracted by other voices peddling a false gospel. Everything that is said and done upholds the communal relationship with the Father, Son, and Spirit, and the community draws on the strength of that relationship to avoid all kinds of evil. When newcomers enter this community, they feel loved, embraced, significant, and new; they are free to be who God has made them to be and to live out the gracious gifts God has given them without constraint or discouragement. This community seeks out those who are broken and lost in darkness, and brings the light of Christ into their lives so that God's Spirit can begin the work of transforming them from the inside out. Having experienced God's transformation in their own lives, they believe and foster the same for others. Their celebration is not induced by substance abuse, but by the sheer joy of living in God's community and the privilege of seeing what God is doing in the lives of others. The source of their joy is that God has brought them from death to life. Aware of their purpose and calling in God's plan to renew the world, members of the community think carefully and methodically on how to make the most of every moment and opportunity to drive back evil by doing good. They are all filled with the Spirit, who brings assurance of God's presence and renewing power to their humanity. United as a community, they live out the light of Christ.

I want to be part of this community! I want to live in love and harmony with others in such a way that everyone's uniqueness is honoured and their contribution unfettered. I want to experience the daily joy of God's Spirit continuing to change me from the inside out, and rejoice over how He is changing others. I want to be part of a community that battles the evil in society, doing good work that promotes the new humanity Jesus achieved for us as a human race. I want to help shine the light that exposes the darkness in the lives of others and makes visible for them the beauty of living in relationship with Father, Son, and Spirit. I know we are not always consistently living and doing this, but we need to reach for it continually. It is the restoration of our full humanity in relationship with God. It is the environment of God's Kingdom come to us in the present. It is the anticipation of, and participation in, the coming dawn of God's renewal and redemption of the world. It is all this that makes God's community the most unique and essential entity in our world; I pray that we never settle for less than this, and never stop reaching for it until Christ returns. It is with that same hope that Paul encourages the Corinthians to "be strong and steady, always enthusiastic about the Lord's work, for you know that nothing you do for the Lord is ever useless."[229]

---

[229] 1 Cor 15:58 (NLT).

Chapter Eight

REDEEMING RELATIONSHIPS

Ephesians 5:22–33

Wives, be to your own husbands as you are to the Lord. The husband is the head of the wife as Christ is the head of God's community, being Himself the Saviour of the body. But as God's community submits to Christ, so wives to their husbands in all things. Husbands, love your wives, just as Christ loves God's community, even as He gave Himself up on her behalf so that He might make her holy, having cleansed her by washing her in water through the word; and that [having done this] He might [also] present her to Himself as a beautiful community, without stain or wrinkle or any such thing, but that she should be holy and blameless.[230] *In this way, husbands owe it to their wives to love them as they love their own bodies. The one who loves his wife loves himself. No man would ever hate his own flesh, but feeds and cares for it, just like Christ with His community. He does this because we belong to His body. Because of this, a man will leave his father and mother and join together with his wife, and the two will become one flesh. This is a great mystery, but I'm talking specifically about Christ and God's community. [Don't miss the point I'm making:] Each one of you [like Christ] should love his wife as he loves himself so that the wife respects her husband.*

HUSBANDS AND WIVES

To understand how truly countercultural Paul's words are in this section of the letter, it is important to know something about the understanding of marriage in first-century Roman culture. Men and women in that context married for the sake of maintaining bloodlines and family status. Among the wealthier, more privileged classes, women were pledged in marriage to male heirs to perpetuate the family name; they were usually married off before reaching puberty, with no choice as to whom they married.[231] Given this reality, very few of the privileged class married for love. These marriages often ended in

---

[230] The same conjunctive phrase is used here as in Eph 1:4, αγιους και αμωμους.

[231] Rodney Stark, *The Triumph of Christianity* (New York: HarperOne, 2011), p. 127.

divorce,[232] as the men were notorious for repeatedly divorcing and remarrying; having used up his wife for what they could gain, "the husband looked for another wife as a stepping stone to a higher place or greater wealth."[233]

Extramarital relationships were common, especially among married men – and, given the behaviour among men, women often followed suit, since they had not married for love in the first place.[234] This created an "extramarital sexual economy",[235] where wealthy Romans looked to their poorer counterparts for such relationships and made it financially advantageous for them to participate. Related to this were the practices of infanticide and abortion, either to discard an unwanted child or to hide the evidence that would uncover an extramarital affair. The female population suffered greatly because of this, and so did the institution of marriage in the Empire; because there was a shortage of females, women were forced to marry young and then remarry repeatedly, due to the death of their much older husbands or because of divorce.[236] This created a highly unstable sense of family in the Empire, where children were born into marriages of convenience and usually experienced the loss of one or more parents early in their childhood. If they were female, they would be engaged to someone very early, before the age of maturity.

In this context, it was typical for husbands to be authoritarian, selfish, neglectful, and mostly absent. Although privileged women had more means at their disposal than poorer ones, all women were defined and limited socially by their gender; women from wealthy families were afforded privileges and education similar to those of their male counterparts, but were identified as "wool-workers",[237] relegated to household duties, and kept from pursuing any public role. Men ruled the realm of politics and civil affairs and women ruled the realm of the household.[238]

---

[232] Will Durant, *The Story of Civilization: Caesar and Christ* (New York: Simon & Schuster, 1972), p. 134. Durant writes, "Adultery was so common as to attract little attention unless played up for political purposes, and practically every well-to-do woman had at least one divorce."

[233] Ibid.

[234] Ross Shepard Kraemer and Mary Rose D'Angelo, *Women and Christian Origins* (Oxford University Press, 1999; EPub file), pp. 31–32.

[235] Ibid., p. 32.

[236] Rodney Stark, *The Triumph of Christianity*, p. 127–128.

[237] Kraemer and D'Angelo, *Women and Christian Origins*, p. 33: "The category of gender, though, was more frequently utilized to elevate another social group – men of all classes – to a separate and superior position. Employing symbolic designations for women as a group, most notably for associating all women with wool-working, was perhaps the most visible way of erasing class distinctions and of positing a domestically defined gender unity among all females."

[238] Rodney Stark, *The Triumph of Christianity*, pp. 122–123. Stark points out that although it is difficult to find a common denominator in terms of practice, Hellenic women for the most

Jewish marriages were also pre-arranged and usually resulted in young women marrying older men. If the woman survived childbirth, she would probably experience several marriages in her lifetime, given that the men in her life would either die or divorce her. She would have received less education, if any, than her male counterparts,[239] and like the Roman women around her she would have been relegated to household duties. However, Jewish women would not have been subjected to infanticide or abortion as often as Roman women were, and consequently had more children.[240] If a well-off Jewish woman was left widowed, with resources willed to her by her late husband, she had a greater degree of influence and management of her own affairs than younger women, unless a guardian had been attached to her by her husband based on family connections. But given Jewish law, it was fair to say that, upon the death of her husband, a Jewish woman would typically be married off to his next-of-kin so as to keep the family within the same tribe, and would be as powerless as before.

All in all, men in the first century, among both Jews and Gentiles, held a vastly superior social position to that of women by virtue of their gender; women had virtually no rights at all and were viewed as inferior. The sense of equality spoken of by Paul in chapter 4 of Ephesians – the equality that properly values difference, including the difference between the sexes – was non-existent in pagan and Jewish culture. But these customs did not altogether escape retaliation and protest on the part of women. Some wealthy women from influential families balked at the societal gender norms and started living out a "new freedom"; rather than giving up their birth family identity to take on their husband's, they kept their birth identity and "moved about almost as freely as men".[241] Some women took up leadership in pagan cults that revolved around female deities;[242] through their involvement as temple priests, they exerted a certain degree of power in the cities where they lived, and played their influence against that of local wealthy men of politics. Other women of lesser means could use sex to entice and wield power over the men who came to them for services. As for children, it has already

part "lived in semi-seclusion", and neither Hellenic nor Roman women had any say as to whom they married, but were to rear children and take care of the household. He also quotes Philo of Alexandria who says that the place of a Jewish woman is "indoors" and that she should keep to herself, being concerned only for the matters in her own household.

[239] Ibid., p. 58.
[240] Ibid., p. 59.
[241] Will Durant, *Caesar and Christ*, p. 134.
[242] Rodney Stark, *The Triumph of Christianity*, p. 123. "…only in a few temples devoted to goddesses were either Roman or Hellenic women allowed to play any significant role in religious life."

been mentioned how cavalier the attitude was as to whether they lived or died. Slaves, too, endured gross inequality and abuse.

In terms of gender roles, then, Roman society was a mess. Men behaved as less than men, and women lost a sense of identity and significance because of it. Trying to find it in other ways, women were lured into the same power plays and scheming as men in order to make their way in life, and it became a culture of vying for control over each other. From the Emperor down to the slave, each person's social identity was based on who had power to control the other; the goal was domination, which usually resulted in the stronger and wealthier taking away from the poorer and less fortunate. In gender relations, it meant that men and women sought to dominate each other for their own selfish purposes, with men generally succeeding and women failing.

Paul presents a very different perspective regarding relationships in society. Rather than domination, Paul focuses on submission. Having become God's community living out the new humanity, believers were to go about all their relationships in a changed way. Relationships were now viewed from an eschatological perspective, according to the reality of God's Kingdom. "It meant the end of life based on hostility, aggression, and repression – life which perpetuated itself by dominating, exploiting, possessing, and manipulating others."[243] The primary point of instruction in this next section of Paul's letter is that God's people, in all sorts of relationships previously characterized by domination, are to function in a submissive manner toward each other. From 5:22 through to 6:9, Paul will describe what submission looks like for each role in each of the foundational relationships that make up society. Contrary to what some have concluded from Paul's parallel passage in Galatians 3:28,[244] it is not that the unique structures expressed in these relationships are to be immediately eliminated, but that they are to be reshaped by the unity and harmony characterizing God's people as Christ transforms them into the new humanity. Since this is a process of "becoming", given the Pauline eschatology in which the Kingdom is here already but also still to be realized, what we are

---

[243] Fred D. Layman, "Male Headship in Paul's Thought," *Wesleyan Theological Journal* 15:1 (Spring 1980), p. 48. Layman further notes, "It meant further elimination of social structures which have served to perpetuate exploitive relationships and to institutionalize subservience of one group to another in the national, racial, economic, religious, and marital orders. *It meant the end of "superior" and "inferior" persons within these orders*" [italics mine]. Eventual elimination of the structures in question would take time; the status of persons within them changed first.

[244] "In Christ's family there can be no division into Jew and non-Jew, slave and free, male and female. Among us you are all equal. That is, we are all in a common relationship with Jesus Christ" (The Message).

talking about is a new order already beginning to penetrate the structures of society with the goal of restoring their true humanity.[245] This way of relating was nothing less than remarkable, given the world that Paul and his readers lived in. It was a radically new way of understanding relationships, unprecedented even in Jewish circles that had the benefit of Torah.[246]

Given the character of the community set forth in chapters 4 and 5 of the letter, Paul now describes what the most important relationships in life look like among those who are "filled with the Spirit" and live out the "fullness" of their new humanity in community. In the final verse of the previous section, Paul characterized the community "filled" with God's Spirit as one where *each submits to the other* out of reverence for Christ. In other words, it is a *mutual* submission among members of God's community, an act of honouring Christ in the new humanity He has given to each person as well as to the community collectively. What follows in this passage are instructions regarding specific "categories of submission",[247] directly tied into that general exhortation to mutual submission as an overarching way of being. In other words, they are descriptions of how each person involved in each of the foundational relationships of society should submit to the other in that relationship.

Some translations use the word "subject"[248] to express both Paul's word for submission in verse 21 and the submission implied but not explicitly mentioned in verse 22. However, the word "subject" has a very monarchical connotation;[249] the inhabitants of a country are "subject" to the monarch that rules over that country. It is a relation based on power and coercion rather than the free self-giving of persons in loving relationship. Paul is writing about something quite different in these verses; he is describing how members of God's community "give themselves" to one another freely and lovingly. If we are to read properly

---

[245] Fred Layman, "Male Headship in Paul's Thought," p. 51.

[246] Ibid., p. 49: "We who stand at the end of three centuries of democracy, two centuries of abolition and labour reform, and a century of women's suffrage and liberation movements cannot feel the full impact and radical sense of newness that Paul's words had with his world, both Jewish and Gentile."

[247] J. David Miller, "Translating Paul's Words about Women," *Stone-Campbell Journal* 12 (2009), p. 70: "Husbands loving wives (5:25, 28, 33) is an example of submission. Wives respecting husbands (5:33) is an example of submission. Children obeying and honouring parents (6:1–2), fathers not exasperating children but raising them in the discipline and instruction of the Lord (6:4), slaves obeying masters (6:5), masters reciprocating with goodwill (6:9) – all these are categories of submission."

[248] Thus, for example, the RSV: "Be subject to one another out of reverence for Christ. Wives, be subject to your husbands, as to the Lord."

[249] As an adjective, it most often means "being dominated by a higher authority."

the exhortations that follow from the general foundation in verse 21, we must keep in mind that the goal of each member is to "give". Everyone gives of themselves based on the role that they play in the community. Wives, the first to be addressed, are asked to be in relationship with their husbands as they are in relationship with Christ (the verb "to be" is missing in the sentence Paul writes, but is directly implied). It is important to note that at this stage of the argument, given verse 21, Paul is invoking "reverence for Christ" as the basis for each partner's mutual submission in relationship, along with that of every believer to every other believer; in other words, our reverent relationship to Christ inspires *all* of us to mutual submission, not only the wife to her husband but the husband to his wife. However, submission will take different forms; in the appeal to the analogy of Christ and His community in the subsequent verses, it is clear that in marriage, the onus will be on the husband to bear the greater weight of the analogy with Christ. For the wife, Paul simply encourages the same kind of "giving" that is the basis of her response to Christ as Lord.

It is important to note what aspects of Christ's example in the analogy are to be applied to the husband and wife relationship. Paul uses the analogy of Christ's headship in relationship to the church to illustrate how the husband is head in relation to his wife. This "headship" is not like the imposing and authoritarian domination practised by men in the surrounding culture; rather, it imitates Jesus in His character as the head of God's community on earth.[250] Paul reminds the listeners that the "headship" Christ holds is on account of His role as Saviour of the community; in that role, Christ gives and empties himself completely – relinquishing His glory, His rights, and His very life (Phil 2:5–8) – in order to save humanity. The husband is charged with the same kind of "headship", expressed in giving himself to and for his wife. Paul continues to expand on the analogy of Christ's headship in the following verses about love (25), self-sacrifice (25), provision (26ff), nourishing (29), and cherishing (29).[251]

It is to this type of "headship" that Paul asks wives to respond in submission. Again, remember that the concept of submission in use here is a free "giving" of oneself to another out of reverence for Christ. In view of this, I believe that where the husband deviates from the character of Christ and in so doing abuses his head-ship, it will result in the wife retreating from submission to such headship. Paul is

---

[250] N. T. Wright, *Paul for Everyone: Prison Letters*, p. 202: "The fascinating thing here is that Paul has a quite different way of going about addressing the problem of gender roles. He insists that the husband should take as his role model, not the typical bossy or bullying male of the modern, or indeed the ancient, stereotype, but Jesus himself."

[251] Fred D. Layman, "Male Headship in Paul's Thought," p. 54.

not promoting subjugation, but rather the self-emptying character of Christ that prompts a voluntary return of commitment on the part of the recipient. One can only be safe in the hands of someone else who is also giving himself. This mutuality is at the core of community among the Persons of the Trinity, and it is what Paul is encouraging as the core of the community among believers.

The role of "headship" in a husband-and-wife relationship is endangered when the husband is not living out of the union of his life with that of Christ. God's heart is for husbands to love their wives as Christ loves God's community. To violate this puts us at odds with God and causes us to work at cross-purposes with what God has given us in Christ.[252] The implication is as basic as Paul's imperative in 5:1 to "be imitators of God, as children who are loved [by their Father]. Live in love just as Christ loved you and gave Himself for us like the sweet-smelling aroma of an offering and a sacrifice to God." As God's community, we are called to imitate the relationship of self-giving inherent in the Trinitarian community, where each gives himself or herself to the other out of love. But we are able to imitate Him only by virtue of our union with Him, our dwelling in Him and His dwelling in us.

It is interesting that in this context of self-giving, Paul also speaks of purifying. In the giving of oneself to another out of love, there is a purifying element that accepts the other as a part of oneself, and in the act of accepting another, one makes the other acceptable. Paul plays on the close tie here between oneness and belonging. In the Jewish context, the concept or ritual of cleansing had attached to it the significance of belonging. A person who, for any of various reasons, was ritually unclean or impure would be marginalized or isolated from the community until restored through a cleansing ritual. Drawing on this analogy, Paul calls on the husband to function as Christ does for humanity, bringing her into full, inclusive relationship with him through his act of self-giving love, so that nothing is allowed to exclude her from that relationship.[253] Like baptism, which welcomes

---

[252] C. Baxter Kruger, *The Great Dance: The Christian Vision Revisited* (Vancouver: Regent College, 2005), p. 95: "We have distinct minds and hearts and wills, but they are minds and hearts and wills that exist in union with God. It is no light matter for our thinking to be in conflict with God's thinking. Such incongruence is a violation, not of some arbitrary and extrinsic divine law, but of our own identity in union with God, and it necessarily causes anguish."

[253] N. T. Wright *Paul for Everyone: Prison Letters*, p. 203–204. "Paul, of course, lived in a world where women were not only regarded as lesser beings but, as often as not, as impure. Their regular bodily functions were deemed to make them dangerous for a man who wanted to maintain his own purity. Paul sees the action of Jesus – and, by the parallel he has set up, the action of the husband – as taking the responsibility to bring the wife into full purity. Instead of rejecting the wife at times of technical 'impurity', the husband is to cherish and take care of her, to look after her and let her know at all times that she is loved and valued."

the convert into the community through the washing or cleansing with water and the affirmation of their faith and commitment in words, so the husband's love reaches out to welcome the wife, declaring her complete acceptability and her deep and permanent connection to him.[254]

In verse 27 Paul reiterates the descriptive couplet "holy and blameless" from 1:4, describing what it is that God does for us through Christ. This is related to the concept of God's adoption and inclusion of humanity into His cosmic family. The family unit of husband and wife is a mirror of that cosmic family, and as the head, the husband makes a point of ensuring the inclusion of his wife through his self-giving love, cherishing, nurturing, and keeping. It is in this way that he reflects the headship of Christ over God's community. Christ's act and goal of "presenting" God's community introduces an eschatological aspect to this as well;[255] the analogous element in marriage is to love in recognition and anticipation of what the other will be, or what the other is eschatologically. In that sense, love also carries with it a sense of hope, believing in the ultimate fulfillment of what Christ has already accomplished for us in His own Person. This kind of love sees, in the limitations of the beloved, what others do not see – what the beloved will become in the end, at the consummation of all things, and in that sense already is.[256] Paul is encouraging the husband to love his wife not only for the present, but also to love her with a view to the future, in anticipation of what she will become and already is in her new humanity.

Verse 28 underlines the equality that exists between husband and wife as Paul emphasizes that a husband's love toward his wife is to be equal to his love for himself. In fact, loving one's wife is the same as loving oneself, reaffirming the reality of oneness between husband and wife. It would be odd and unnatural for a man to treat himself with hatred or indifference. Rather, a man takes care of himself. Nurturing and caring for his wife is equivalent to taking care of himself, and reflects the way that Christ cares for God's community. Paul confirms the

---

[254] F. F. Bruce, *Epistle to the Colossians to Philemon and to the Ephesians* (Grand Rapids, MI: Eerdmans, 1984), pp. 388–389. Bruce sees "washing and word" as part and parcel of the ritual of baptism indicating the commitment of a convert to Christ and their inclusion into the "new society".

[255] Frank E. Gaebelein, ed., *The Expositor's Bible Commentary*, vol. 11 (Grand Rapids, MI: Zondervan, 1981), p. 77. "The ultimate aim in view when Christ gave himself up for the church (v. 25) was that at the end of the age he might be able to present her to himself in unsullied splendor ..."

[256] In light of this, love can accept the limitations of the present because of the knowledge of what is to come, the implication being that what we see in each other in the present points toward the future of our becoming in Christ. This is a very important aspect of love in relationships that are characterized by the Spirit's presence in our life.

connection with the analogy by stating that as God's community we "belong" to Christ as members of the same organism, or in Paul's words, the same "body". Again, oneness and belonging.

Paul expands on this concept of "body" by declaring that we are of Christ's "flesh and bones". Certainly this is a reference to the connection between man and woman in the creation story in Genesis: when Eve is brought to Adam, he exclaims, "This at last is bone of my bones, and flesh of my flesh!" (Gen 2:23) They literally come from the same flesh and bone: God fashioned the woman from the man. The two essentially belong together, and because of this belonging, a man will leave his family in search of a woman to whom he belongs, and the two will become "one flesh". Like Jesus, who left his "home" where he dwelt with the Father and the Spirit in order to give himself for the sake of restoring humanity to relationship with Him, so the man will leave his family to give himself in commitment to a relationship with his wife.[257] Paul then makes sure that the analogy is not taken off on a tangent concerning the man coming first and being superior, as the readers may be tempted to do. He clarifies that he is not talking about Adam and Eve, in fact, but about Christ and God's community. In other words, the emphasis is on what marriage looks like in God's community. As in other relationships, on which Paul will soon comment as well, those who participate in marriage relationships should conduct them with an attitude of love and mutual submission because they *belong to each other*, not only as spouses but at an even more fundamental level in their very humanity. How do they know they belong to each other? They belong to one another by virtue of Christ's bringing them into one new humanity, where there is no longer hostility but rather peace, harmony, unity, and love. In marriage, the husband has the task of nourishing this connection through his self-giving love for his wife, like the self-giving love of Christ for humanity. Because they belong to each other, essentially being of the same flesh, the husband should love his wife as he loves himself.

To develop this concept further: it may seem odd that Paul invokes the reality of self-love to argue for the importance of a husband loving his wife, but when put into the context of God's community and its relationship to Him, the idea becomes clear. In giving the community a new humanity, Christ causes that humanity to love what He has given; when we read in this letter about how wonderful the new humanity is, our response should be to love what Christ gives,

---

[257] Fred D. Layman, "Male Headship in Paul's Thought," p. 54: "As Christ left His Father's house to take up obedient submission (Phil. 2:6, 8), so the husband must leave the home of his parents and enter a relationship of commitment and mutual subjection with his wife (vs. 21, 33). In this way man and wife parallel the mystery of Christ and the Church (v. 32)."

as it is His own nature in us. Christ loves his "body", that is, God's community, as God's Spirit is present in that "body"; it would be strange for Him not to love His "body", God's community, when it is indwelt by Himself and the third Person of the Trinity, along with God's own creation in the form of humanity. In this sense, love of self in God's community is a reflection of our love for God. We tend not to speak this way, because there is always the potential for distortion into narcissism, but the reality is that our love for each other in God's community is a love for God and for ourselves. Loving one's wife as one's own flesh is then natural for one who belongs to God's community.

The final sentence in verse 33 is quite interesting as well. Literally, Paul writes, "…let the wife respect her husband." The word meaning "fear" or "awe" is the same word that Paul uses in verse 21 as the motivation of our submission to one another: we do so out of "reverence" for Christ.[258] Fear is non-existent in God's community, since its relationship is with a God whose very nature is love, expressed in the fellowship of Father, Son, and Spirit, and love and fear are mutually exclusive. In a context of love, "fear" is actually "reverence". When a husband loves his wife the way Christ loves God's community, then she will have "reverence" or "respect" for him because of his move of including her in his life and very being. She will not fear him, but will regard him highly because of his love. Should that love *not* be there, she would indeed have much to fear, such as the absence of nurture and care.[259] There was certainly much for the wife to fear in the typical marriage in the Empire, as these relationships were not based on such love. In a marriage within God's community, however, the wife can give her husband the same kind of reverence she has for Christ and His self-giving if the husband gives in the same way.

As a point of application, it's important to see that Paul puts the onus on the man in the marriage relationship to initiate the caring and nurture of the wife. The husband takes the lead on this. Since he came first and the woman

---

[258] Colin Brown, ed., *The New International Dictionary of New Testament Theology*, vol. 1 (Grand Rapids, IL: Zondervan, 1975), p. 622–624. The article indicates that the φoβεω word group is used in the NT to mean fear, reverence, or awe. It is used of a Christian's relationship with God or Christ as "reverence", as in Eph 5:21. The article also interestingly notes that in the NT there is a "tension between fear and love. In a paradoxical way they exist together." In view of 1 John 4:18, the only kind of fear that can exist together with love is reverence. Since the context in this part of the Ephesian letter is love – husband for wife and Christ for the church – we can conclude that the relationship in question is characterized by reverence. If love is absent, the implication is that the reverence turns to fear. A god who does not love is to be feared. A man who does not love will be feared by his wife.

[259] There is no evidence that Paul actually makes a play on the dual meaning of φoβεω, but being the type of writer he is, it may be lurking behind this statement he makes.

came from him, he should be first in leading them toward growth and health as a couple. There is nothing authoritarian about such leadership. In a culture that prides itself on "liberation" from traditional gender roles, we find that the result leaves much to be desired.[260] Those who criticize Paul for still being too traditional should take a good look at what the relationship of husbands and wives has become in our day and age. The tabloids are filled with a messed-up view of marriage among the wealthy and famous; very few well-known marriages actually survive our society's lack of moral focus, which is only intensified by the stresses of fame and power. Many other people let these high-profile examples influence their own marriages and so lose any faith in the relationship. Meanwhile there is also confusion about gender roles, and about gender specifically. Men have lost track of what it is to be men, and because of this women have lost their own identity as well.

But in God's community, the equality among members honours both unity and diversity. In this community, the diversity between genders is honoured especially in marriage as it is lived out in the new humanity; here the role of the male is to behave and act in sacrificial love towards the female as Christ does toward God's community, and the role of the female is to receive this with trusting love and reverence in the same way that God's community responds to Christ. When the two commit to one another, they enhance their gender identity and role while defining the most intimate mutual submission of any relationship found in society. Where we falter is in following the lead of our morally bankrupt society rather than the biblical reality of community and marriage. A strong marriage that is rooted in God's community is able to ward off all kinds of evil that seeks to undermine it. With such strong marriages, we can shine a light that exposes the darkness of others in regard to marriage and awakens them to what God has intended and given for men and women in the new humanity.

Ephesians 6:1–4

Children, listen to your parents in the Lord; it's the right thing to do. Honour your father and mother, which is the commandment, the first to come with a

---

[260] N. T. Wright, *Paul for Everyone: Prison Letters*, p. 205: "If this guideline still seems outrageous in today's culture, we should ask ourselves: do our modern societies, in which marriage is often a tragedy or a joke, really offer a better model of how to do it? Does the spectre of broken homes littering modern Western culture indicate that we've got it right and can tell the rest of human history how we finally resolved the battle of the sexes? Or does it indicate that we still need to do some rethinking somewhere?"

promise: that it might go well for you and that you might have a long life.[261]
Fathers especially, don't push your children to anger, but guide them with
instruction and discipline in keeping with how the Lord does it.

CHILDREN AND PARENTS

Paul continues to describe what relationships in God's community look like by
addressing that of children and parents. Remembering 5:21 as the controlling
verse that defines how each member of a relationship gives himself or herself
to the other, we can expect that these next instructions will detail the kind of
submission to be shown by children and by parents respectively towards each
other.

The form taken by submission on the part of children is to "listen" to their
parents. Paul qualifies the statement by attaching the modifying phrase "in the
Lord". At first glance one might suspect that Paul is instructing children to listen
only to parents who are "in the Lord", that is, parents who are believers; but on
a closer look at the sentence and context, it makes more sense that "in the Lord"
is modifying both "listening" and "parents".[262] In this way Paul is pointing out
that the act of "listening" should occur in a way that sees the relationship in the
context of Christ, as part of the life of both children and parents in Christ. In
other words, in the eschatological reality of true community that has come in the
new humanity given by Christ, children are to view their parents in the loving
equality and acceptance that characterizes that community. In so doing, they
view their parents not only as they are but also as what they will become. Echoes
of what Paul wrote earlier at the beginning of chapter 4 of the letter, of "being
patient" and "putting up with each other", are sounded in the implications of
this verse. Both children and parents are on the road to learning to live in the
new humanity. This means that neither has arrived at "fullness" but both have
the "fullness" of the Spirit available to them to sustain and guarantee their growth
into living out the new humanity.

This is an important distinction, because certainly some of the hearers of
this letter had miserable parents. Knowing the culture of the Empire, in which

---

[261] I did not include the words "on the earth." But I do want to point out that this prepositional
phrase confirms that long life is not spiritual eternal existence (although that is ours in Christ as
well) but a long life lived out on earth.

[262] Frank Gaebelein, *The Expositor's Bible Commentary*, vol. 11, p. 82. Commentator Skevington
Wood clarifies that "If the phrase εν κυριω (*en kyrio*, "in the Lord") is original (it is not read
by some authorities), it is more naturally attached to υπακουετε (*hypakouete*, "obey") than
to γονευσιν (*goneusin*, "parents") or to both. It indicates the sphere in which the Christian's
obedience operates and perhaps also the spirit in which it is yielded."

children had virtually no rights, some would have been disowned by their parents, and some possibly even left as infants on the trash heaps and rescued by adoptive parents. Many others would have suffered some form of brutality and were now perhaps left with the burden of caring for their brutal parents in their old age. Whatever the situation, whether parents are believers or not, children are to offer a listening ear to them in keeping with how God desires the relationship to function – in the mutually submissive attitude of love and acceptance. For someone struggling to love parents who historically have not loved back, being able to listen to those parents comes from viewing them not as they are, but as what Christ is making them to be in God's community. This is a way of honouring their humanity and what Christ has given, even though they have not lived out their parenthood based on the new humanity.

As well, there is a direct connection of the above to the next line in the letter, where Paul encourages children to "honour" their father and mother. First of all, he cites it as being a commandment.[263] For that matter, it is the fifth commandment in the list of ten in Exodus 20, and the first to have a promise attached. Paul's point here is that this act of honouring one's parents is not only directly ordained by God from the earliest days of His covenant with His people, but also has attached to it His promise that anyone who does so has a good chance of living a long life. In a very real sense, "honouring" has been the substance of Paul's message throughout the letter. We have heard Paul describe God the Father honouring His creation by rescuing and redeeming it, Christ honouring the will of the Father by giving Himself for our sake, the Spirit honouring the work of Christ in our lives by continuing to mold and shape us from the inside out, and we as God's community honouring one another by our mutual submission, in keeping with the new humanity that God has honoured us with. Paul simply continues this theme of "honouring" in one more commandment, reiterating to children that "honouring" is the appropriate way to relate to parents in God's community. It is "the right thing to do" not only because they are fellow participants in the new humanity, but because they have been the instruments of God in creating life; they are the vehicles through whom we now find ourselves alive and able to take part in the new humanity given to us by Christ.

Parents in God's community, especially fathers, also have an obligation to submit to their children – though not, of course, in such a way as to allow their children to walk over them and so dishonour them as parents. Submission is

---

[263] Do not let the word "first" throw you off. If you read the commandments in Exodus 20, you will see that it is the first commandment that has a promise attached. Paul's word order in the sentence at the end of verse 2 is "which is [the]commandment, first with a promise."

never about that, and in any case Paul has just finished commanding children to listen to and honour their parents. No, submission on the part of fathers takes the form of gentleness, of respect for who their children are, of discipline that seeks the good of their children rather than their own convenience or comfort, or the fulfillment of their own dreams. Fathers do not have the right to frustrate their children so as to cause them to retaliate in anger. That is a capricious, demanding attitude on the part of a parent and is not in keeping with the mutually submissive attitudes we are to show toward each other out of reverence for Christ. I must admit, as a father myself, that fathers often have a tendency to be hard on their children in a way that mothers are not. More often, mothers seem to have an immediate nurturing connection with their children; after all, at one time they were of "one flesh" – they carried their children in their own bodies and gave birth to them. Fathers miss that connection and tend to err in feeling that discipline and busyness will create character. They do, in fact, but as fathers we tend to take this too far. Some things do not change over the centuries, and Paul's admonition to fathers to "lay off" their children in exchange for raising them God's way has direct application to our context as well. Paul is not suggesting that fathers be wishy-washy pushovers, always giving kids their own way. Rather, he encourages fathers to teach and discipline their children, not in the authoritarian, domineering, coercive model of the culture of the Empire, but in the way that God goes about it. Think of the incredible love and patience God showed toward Israel over the centuries and, for that matter, continues to show to humanity in general and to each of us who call Him Father. Instructing and advising, warning and correcting, waiting patiently, forgiving and restoring, being there for us – these are the ways that God has displayed His loving character as He has historically engaged in relationship with humanity. Yes, God is firm, and even allows His children to suffer the consequences of their disobedience, but always in the context of love and a desire that they become what He has created them to be.

I want to emphasize "in keeping with how the Lord does it" (vs. 4). Relationships can be lived out in two ways. We can be influenced by society and culture, and so assume the common practice that leaves wanting a true reflection of the triune God of grace and His design for such relationships, or we can live them out in keeping with God's character and desire, and so bring Him honour and pleasure. Going right back to the beginning of the letter, God takes pleasure in rescuing humanity and restoring it to relationship with Him. He also takes great pleasure in the work of His Son, who gives a new humanity to Jews and

Gentiles so that they can exist in a community of love, harmony, and peace. God takes extreme pleasure in seeing us take the new humanity given by Christ and, by the Spirit's help and power, live out our relationships in a way that builds up the other and encourages further growth in that new humanity. We have a conscious choice every day in how we will live. If we are not intentional about this choice, we will neglect living as God's community and perpetuate the old humanity. And if we do that long enough, we can slip into the darkness of the past and forget what life is like in the "Father's house".

Evil would like nothing better than to undermine the relationships in families between parents and children, and is doing a fairly good job of this in many cases in our culture today. Living out the new humanity in our families is important for our own sakes and for the sake of our present society. Let's not forget that all this "relating" is part of living as children of light! That light is desperately needed in the world of darkness where so many others continue to live.

Ephesians 6:5–9

Slaves, listen to your earthly masters with fear and trembling, as you would focus your heart [on listening] to Christ. Don't just work to please others as though someone were watching you, but as heartfelt slaves of Christ, doing what God desires of you, provide service with a good will as though you are doing it for the Lord and not for men. Know that whatever good thing each one does, the Lord will give the same in return, whether they are a slave or a freedman. Masters, do the same in return for your slaves. Stop [trying to motivate them by] threatening them. Remember that you both have the same Master who is in heaven. He has no bias.

SLAVES AND MASTERS

Some people reading this section of the letter may wonder how it applies to our context, seeing as there have been no slaves in Western culture for the last two centuries. Some who feel this way have altered the reference and contemporized the language by referring to employees and employers; in the past I have done this myself in order to make this section more relevant for us. But having since delved much more deeply into the world of slaves in the first century, I believe it is important to pay attention to what Paul says specifically with regard to relationships between slaves and masters, and see how it bears on the general theme of mutual submission that runs through this section of the letter. To pass immediately to a contemporized version of the relationship is to miss the impact of what Paul is saying.

The Roman Empire literally ran on slave power. The great feats of architecture and engineering were all carried out by slaves. If there was a need to move tons of stone from one place to another, the Romans had slaves that could do it. It was a way of life and culture that no one dared question or change. It is estimated that at the height of its operation, the Empire needed to find 500,000 new slaves each year to maintain its infrastructure.[264] These slaves were acquired through the conquest of distant lands, where the Romans subjugated nations and people groups and took back human beings as spoils of war that would live out the rest of their days in slavery. It would be easy to criticize Paul here for continuing to accept such treatment of humanity in his culture. The problem is that we are not fully aware of the degree to which slavery was a part of his world. N. T. Wright puts it this way:

> The answer is that Paul could no more envisage a world without slavery than we can envisage a world without electricity. Most of what the modern world takes for granted – television, computers, and a million lesser inventions – are impossible without electricity. And yet for most of human history it was unknown. In the same way, the way Paul's world worked was through slaves taking a vital place in most households except the very poor. ... [T]hey were simply part of the way the world worked. In this area at least, Paul was not starting from scratch and attempting to design a new way for the world to run. Everyone would be liberated from every form of slavery, in the age to come; but in a world where many Christians were slaves working for non-Christian masters it was worse than useless to suggest instant emancipation. Paul wisely chooses a different route.[265]

Paul begins addressing the injustice of the treatment of slaves by encouraging a different kind of behaviour in both parties. Rather than call for a complete and immediate abolition of slavery, Paul is calling the relationship to a higher standard, one in keeping with the character of relationships that exist in God's community generally. This is the approach that would slowly trickle through the Christian community in the first and second centuries AD and be assimilated into the consciousness of the Empire. The church did, in time, begin to speak out

---

[264] Jeffrey A. Winters, *Oligarchy* (Cambridge University Press, 2011; EPub file), p. 120.
[265] N. T. Wright, *Paul for Everyone: Prison Letters*, p. 215.

against slavery both in word and deed; the decline of the Empire is attributed in part to the church's move in recognizing slaves as equal with other human beings. As the church continued to extend its reach and acceptance to slaves, offering them full inclusion in their communities as brothers and sisters in Christ, it became more difficult to maintain slavery as an institution and necessity. This slow but steady move began forcing the wealthy to hire more and more free men to do their work.[266] It also created a climate in which slave owners were more apt to grant freedom to their slaves and employ them as workers.

One of the lessons to be learned from this is the importance of choosing where to fight the battle against evil in society. Paul shows that beginning to address attitudes and behaviour is more conducive to change than trying to coerce the adjustment of cultural norms by influencing legislation.[267] Here he urges God's community towards a change in attitude and behaviour so that these relationships carry on with a different character and focus. The result can be seen in the effect the church had over time on the view of slaves in the Empire.

In this section of the letter, Paul begins by addressing the form of submission that slaves should adopt in relationship to their masters. They are to "listen", or, as some other translations put it, "obey" their masters. But the character of this submission is not merely to do the will of the master. Paul sets a higher expectation on slaves in terms of attitude or manner: they are to go about serving their masters *as if they were serving their Lord, Jesus Christ*. Remembering what we have already said about the different meanings of "fear" in connection with the verses about "reverence for Christ" (5:21) and wives respecting their husbands (5:33), it is worth noting that the phrase "fear and trembling" in verse 5 of our current passage is also used by Paul in Philippians 2:12. There, he uses it in reference to the attitude believers ought to have while "working out" their salvation: they do so in the knowledge that God is present and involved. In that passage Paul is urging his listeners, now that he is physically absent from them, to continue to follow his advice as they did in the past when he was among them; it is an act of obedience to God.[268] In the same way, the "fear and trembling" of slaves, as they take care to listen to their masters, is a recognition of the reality of Christ's presence and involvement in the relationship, an understanding that

---

[266] Rodney Stark, *The Victory of Reason: How Christianity Led to Freedom, Capitalism, and Western Success* (New York: Random House, 2005), pp. 28–32.

[267] This would have been especially true with an issue such as slave ownership in the first century, which was embedded into the very fabric of that society.

[268] "Dearest friends, you were always so careful to follow my instructions when I was with you. And now that I am away you must be even more careful to put into action God's saving work in your lives, obeying God with deep reverence and fear" (NLT).

their service is really to Him. Echoes of Ephesians 5:21 continue here: it is out of "reverence for Christ" that the slave is encouraged to submit to his master. In the parallel verse in Colossians 3:22, Paul writes this same advice with a very explicit reference to Christ: "Obey them [i.e., your masters] willingly because of your reverent fear of the Lord" (NLT).

Thus the standard of relationship is raised from slave and master to slave and Christ. The way to respond in loving submission to a master, from a slave's point of view, is to do the will of the master as coming from the Lord himself. This approach produces a very different outcome: the work of the slave is no longer to satisfy those who are looking on as supervisors, nor is it the slave's objective to get away with doing the minimum, to do as little work as required while still managing to carry out the master's will. The slave works for the master in order to serve and please the Lord.

What echoes in the background is Ephesians 2:10: "We are his masterpiece, created in Christ Jesus to do good works in keeping with how God intended for us to live." As discussed earlier in relation to this verse, Paul is describing the ideal role of humanity in the creation.[269] God created us as his "work of art" to enhance life on earth. When we do our work for God – and this applies to employees as well as slaves – we are not only working for others but working to enhance the world around us. Our work is more than just to provide us a living; it is to contribute to the great harmony and creativity of the world that God put us in. By working with this in view, we bring more life to everything around us.

There is much to gain in return, says Paul, when we do our work this way. When we give out of our good will in our work for others, as service to the Lord, God Himself will give to us in return. There is a reward for anyone who seeks to work toward the enhancement of the world around them: God has embedded this in the order of creation. Look at the fruit of hard work that gives more to others than just selfish gain. Those who work in this way make the world better for those they work and live with, and also find their work fulfilling.

The other aspect of this is that relating to the master in light of what the master will become in God's gift of new humanity actually allows the slave to impart grace. Masters were brutal in Paul's day. But a slave who showed his master loving, voluntary submission, in recognition of their joint participation in the new humanity given by Christ, made it possible for the master to recognize their shared dignity in Christ's new humanity, and act accordingly. We have the

---

[269] See page 30 of this book, "Rather than living out the works of death that characterize our former zombie-like existence, destroying ourselves and others, we have received at God's hands the gift of living a life of goodness that, in turn, brings more life to the rest of creation."

ability, given to us by God through His Spirit, to help others who are in darkness to see themselves as far more than they presently are. By so doing, we raise their level of consciousness and awareness of what they are, and what those around them are, in Jesus Christ. It is in this way that slaves can "awaken" their masters and "open their eyes" to their true identity in Christ.

Paul then instructs masters in how they are to demonstrate submission in the relationship. Masters are to return the same attitude to their slaves. If the slave is to serve his master in the way he would serve the Lord, the master's role is to behave toward his slave as our Lord treats us. He should relate to his slaves in a way that acknowledges the presence and involvement of Christ in the relationship, understanding that when he honours his slave, he honours Christ. As the slave gives to his master, so the master should give in return. This fulfills the mutual submission that is to characterize all relationships in God's community.

Paul accordingly advises masters not to abuse the relationship by taking an authoritarian stance and lording it over their slaves on the grounds of their superior position. In God's community, no one is superior to any other, but in their diversity all are equal and share in a relationship of mutual submission. The master should apply his resources to enhance the life of his slave, while the slave applies what he or she has to give to enhance the life of the master. The use of threats in order to get slaves to perform, so common in the surrounding culture, is demeaning and does not honour true humanity.

In the Empire, the wealthy were always concerned that their slaves could at any moment rise up against them in numbers. They sought to prevent this by using tactics to enforce subjugation and maintain their authority and control through terrorization. What kept slaves in line was the threat of punishment or death should they attempt to revolt or retaliate against their master.[270] Paul is urging slave owners to take a different approach in their relationships with their slaves. Rather than continue the societal norm of control and domination, Paul encourages them to act out of a perspective of equality with their slaves before

---

[270] Jeffrey Winters, *Oligarchy*, pp. 106–108. Winters quotes a famous Roman proverb: "So many slaves, so many foes." He describes how, out of necessity, oligarchs in the Empire worked at "psychologically and physically" defeating their slaves in order to avert the serious threat they were perceived to pose. The whole atmosphere of relationship between slaves and landowners was exacerbated by the monopolization of ownership of land by the elite, so that even soldiers returning from lengthy service abroad were forced into slave labour upon their return. This created an extreme division and sense of resentment between rich and poor that came to a climax during the reign of Julius Caesar. See Simon Baker, *Ancient Rome: The Rise and Fall of an Empire* (BBC Books, 2007; EPub file), especially the chapter "Revolution", for a narrative of the mounting unrest among plebeians.

God – to treat them according to the value of humanity that God has placed on them both.

Paul levels the playing field when it comes to master-slave relationships by emphasizing that both master and slave have Christ as their Lord. The master is not an authority unto himself to do as he pleases; rather, his position in life is afforded to him by God, and so he answers to God for how he treats others. Slaves are similarly responsible to God for how they treat their masters. God does not play favourites. There is no biased appreciation by God of one over the other; God loves all equally. Paul has already established that the redemptive work of Christ recovers *all humanity*; He does not show partiality. In chapter 2 of the letter, Paul made it clear that God gathers both Jews and Gentiles together into one new humanity; neither is given preference over the other, but both are equal recipients of God's saving grace, forgiveness, and loving renewal. Paul makes this his main point in the letter to the Romans as well. The two groups, Jews and Gentiles, were arguing about which of them was more loved by God, and Paul makes it very clear that there is no boasting whatsoever in one's personal pedigree, position, or national identity. The controlling verse that establishes this is Romans 11:32, where Paul says, "God has imprisoned all people in their own disobedience so that he could have mercy on them all" (NLT). It is against this background that Paul establishes equality in working relationships here in Ephesians, by noting that both parties have obligations to God and to one another that demand honouring each other's humanity.

As a final word on this section, it is clear by now that Paul's goal in this letter is to affirm what God desires and has accomplished in Jesus Christ and through His Spirit in the lives of human beings, and to explain the implications of this for those who have been given new humanity. We are destined for nothing less than living as a cohesive, loving community where the attitude is one of unselfish giving to each other that produces growth and maturity. The community is at its best when it lets the Spirit work in it, and in each individual, to help all assume the character of Christ. What God desires for this renewed community is that they live out their unity-in-diversity in the mutual submission that characterizes the triune community of Father, Son, and Spirit. The beauty of such relationship is transforming, and shines the light of God and His character onto the world so that the world sees its own need, sees what God desires and is able to accomplish in each person's life, and responds.

Paul will now go on to talk about how, in addition to the privilege of bringing His light to those in the darkness, God has given this community the opportunity to fight alongside Him against evil in the world. God's final goal is to purge the world of all evil.[271] In His wisdom He has given us understanding so that we can live out our new humanity in His community, showing forth His character in relationships that dispel both darkness and evil so that evil can be battled in earnest without threat of failure. God will win in the end. In the meantime, he is working through us as His community to battle alongside Him against the relentless forces of evil attempting to plunge humanity further into darkness. But we can't fight evil unless we do so together as His community.

All that Paul has said so far, he has said in order to be able to share what comes next in chapter 6 of the letter.[272] Relationships in God's community have a redeeming quality that exerts a powerful effect in the world, giving the world a picture of what humanity is like when it is connected to God. Living in loving relationship is how we thrive, and how we communicate God's light to the world; it is also the ground out of which we prepare ourselves to join God in fighting against evil.

---

[271] See Rev 21 for the final state of creation in fulfillment of God's desire for it.

[272] I owe this thought to Rikk Watts of Regent College Vancouver, who made this very clear statement in a lecturing recording that was heard by a very ripe and ready heart.

Chapter Nine

BATTLING EVIL

Ephesians 6:10–18

Finally, be strong in the Lord and in the strength of his power. Put on God's full outfit for battle so you'll be able to stand against the tricks of the devil. Our wrestling is not against fellow humans, but against heads, powers, and world rulers of our dark days and against the spiritual forces of evil in the heavens. Put on the whole armour of God so that you'll be able to stand against the evil day and do everything you can to stand. The way to stand is with the truth buckled around your waist, righteousness as your breastplate, and your feet ready to spread[273] the Good News of Peace. Covering all of it is the shield of faith so you'll be able to extinguish the fiery arrows of the evil one. Take the helmet of salvation and the sword of the Spirit, which is God's word, and with all your requests in hand, keep praying always in the Spirit. In this [way] stay awake with all perseverance and prayer for all the holy ones.

GETTING PREPARED

The way Paul begins this last section of the letter gives the impression that (as I suggested earlier) everything he has written so far was intended to lead to this specific outcome, and that here at last is the thing he wants his listeners to grasp.[274] The strength for God's community comes from God; there is no way anybody can fight evil independently. It's not a battle fought on battlefields with artillery, weapons, strength of numbers, and brute force. In fact, that kind of war only aids and abets evil, for evil rejoices over physical destruction. Evil rejoiced over the obliteration of the Carthaginian people at the hands of the Romans. It loves to see humanity do itself in. It is said that when the Roman general looked

---

[273] I decided to keep the choice of verb consistent with feet in terms of how the Good News is conveyed. Paul mixes metaphors, attaching "announcing" to "feet". My use of "spreading" the Good News of Peace is an effort to keep the action consistent with "feet", realizing that "announcing" would be one of the implications of "spreading".

[274] Gordon D. Fee, *God's Empowering Presence*, p. 723: "Given the nature of ancient rhetoric, in coming to this final section of the letter we also most likely are coming to Paul's primary concern for his recipients. That is, Paul's placing this material in the emphatic final position suggests that he has been intentionally building the letter toward this climax right along."

over the city of Carthage, smoldering in ruins after it was sacked, raped, and pillaged by his men, he broke into tears. When asked why he was shedding tears and not rejoicing over the triumph, he answered that he feared Rome would one day suffer the same fate.[275] This is the kind of war evil rejoices over, where even the victors continue in their insecurity and fear knowing that their greed and power will also be their undoing.

The battle Paul is focusing on is fought on a different field. The enemy lurks behind the scenes, ever seeking to undermine creation and the true humanity that Christ has given. Weapons of war are useless against this enemy, who is the archrival of God and His creation. He is the evil one; Paul calls him the devil. His goal is to turn out the lights in the heart and soul of every human being, and his strategy is to distance men and women from each other and from God. He knows that this will cause them to turn from the light of God's truth and be plunged into darkness. He leads his captives into the dark and gets them hooked on all kinds of things that will keep them there.[276]

This battle can be fought only with gear that comes from God himself; it's the only way we can stand a chance against such a vile foe. The enemy is devious, and comes with a boatload of tricks to disguise its presence, even managing to pass itself off as light;[277] we don't even realize we are in the enemy's territory until it is too late. To battle this enemy and avoid succumbing to its craftiness, the believer needs to be outfitted by God and learn a new way of wrestling.[278] There is only One who can teach such an ancient art, and that is the One who has already defeated this enemy and therefore knows both the type of armour and the technique needed.

Some believe that, while writing this passage, Paul was looking at one of the soldiers guarding him and was trying to make analogies between conventional

---

[275] Simon Baker, "Revolution", in *Ancient Rome: The Rise and Fall of an Empire* (BBC Books, 2007; EPub file), p. 36.

[276] C. Baxter Kruger, *The Great Dance*, p. 70: "The evil one is limited to the possibility of perverting or distorting or poisoning our participation in the Triune life. And he cannot do that without our permission, without our decision, without our choice. His strategy is to confuse us so that we unwittingly, yet willfully, work and act against our participation in the great dance of life. His sphere of operation is the irreducible "you" and specifically, your mind. His schemes are calculated to deceive. And the exact target of his schemes is our understanding of who we are, our identity."

[277] 2 Cor 11:14. "Even Satan can disguise himself as an angel of light" (NLT).

[278] Michael E. Gudorf, "The Use of *Pale* in Ephesians 6:12", *Journal of Biblical Literature* 117:2 (Summer 1998), p. 334. According to Gudorf, the specific use of πάλη by Paul is to suggest the type of fighting that includes the cunning of wrestling. "Describing the 'battle' being waged with the word πάλη in v. 12 rather than with what one would normally expect in the context, namely, μάχη (or even ἀγων), helps evoke in the reader's mind the concept not only of standing but also that of standing against a cunning opponent in a close-quarter struggle."

Roman armour and the types of "spiritual" weapons that are needed for the fight against evil. Most scholars who take this view rely heavily on the Hellenic-Roman context in which Paul lived, but not on his Jewish background. However, if we understand how deeply Paul is embedded in Jewish culture and history, we might expect that this battle gear is described somewhere in the Jewish Scriptures he was using: the Old Testament. The God of Israel has been the longest-standing opponent of evil throughout history – right from its inception as described in the biblical story of origins, where God at once identified His intention to deal decisively with the evil that had already begun to undermine His creation.

The most likely source for Paul's description of God's armour is the book of Isaiah, which focuses on God's cosmic plan for rescuing humanity and the earth. The prophet gives pertinent information about this plan, which God has prompted him to share with Israel, instructing the people to tear down the high places where they were sacrificing to gods made by their own hands and warning them that continuing in this idolatrous way would lead to their destruction. He tells Israel that God is preparing a way back to Him, and that the way to receive it is through repentance, humility, openness, honesty, and patience. The God of Israel is not capricious, like the gods of other nations; He is a reasonable God. He wears His armour and wages war to make His name known to the nations, so that others may follow and worship Him. God calls Israel to resume its role as light to the nations; this is the kind of offering that He will accept from them. And He will raise up His Faithful Servant among them to heal them and to lead the way, making His name famous. Through this, God will restore His presence both in Israel and in the world.

The author of the book of Isaiah portrays a "Divine Warrior King", who is either a persona assumed by God Himself or another character who fights on God's behalf. God takes the characteristics of this Divine Warrior King and gives them by His Spirit to the prophet as well. Isaiah 11 tells of the hope of a coming warrior who will fight for Israel, a descendant of David upon whom the Spirit of God will rest.[279]

The armour of God described by Paul, to be taken on by God's community, is drawn partly from this imagery in Isaiah 11. The reference to the "sword of

---

[279] William N. Wilder, "The Use (or Abuse) of Power in High Places: Gifts Given and Received in Isaiah, Psalm 68, and Ephesians 4:8", *Bulletin for Biblical Research* 20:2 (2010), pp. 190–191. Wilder suggests that Paul's borrowing of the Isa 11 idea of the impartation of the power of the Divine Warrior King figure is particularly evident in Eph 1:17 with the giving of the Spirit of wisdom and understanding – the same wisdom and understanding possessed by the Messianic Branch. "That this is Paul's intention is confirmed in Eph. 6:10–20, in which he exhorts believers to put on the full armour of God and then proceeds to enumerate the pieces of that armour in terms drawn in part from the continuing description of the Messianic Branch in Isa 11."

the Spirit", for example, representing "God's word", finds a parallel in the "word of his mouth" and "the breath of his lips", used by the Divine Warrior King figure (the Messianic "branch") to judge the earth.[280] Paul may also be drawing on Isaiah 49:2 for this, where the prophet describes his "words of judgment" as a "sharp sword" in his mouth given him by God so that he might become a "sharp arrow in God's quiver". In the immediate context of Isaiah 49:2, God is affirming to the prophet that he has set him apart so that he will help not only to "restore the people of Israel" but also to enable it to be a "light to the Gentiles, bringing His salvation to the ends of the earth."[281] Paul most likely combined these Isaianic references to encourage his listeners to take God's words and use them as a weapon – a sword, so to speak – that will cut through the deception and darkness of evil to bring salvation.[282]

The Isaiah 11 passage could also be Paul's source for encouraging readers of the letter to "buckle up truth" around their waist. According to Wilder in his exposition of these parallels, "The righteousness and truth (αληθεια) with which the Branch is girded (εξωσμενος) in Isaiah 11:5 appears as the truth (αληθεια) with which one is girded (περιζωσαμενοι) in Ephesians 6:14."[283]

From Isaiah 59 come two other pieces of the armour Paul describes, worn by God himself as He descends to the earth to fight for justice for the poor and marginalized. The chapter begins with the prophet drawing attention to Israel's inability to do right as a community because of its sin. God, who sees and is angered by this, descends and fights for those who have no defender,[284] and the armour He wears in this fight consists of the "breastplate of righteousness" and the "helmet of salvation." God is fighting in this passage because evil has been

---

[280] Ibid., p. 190. See also Paula Qualls and John D. Watts, "Isaiah in Ephesians", *Review and Expositor* 93 (1996), p. 256: "Isaiah does not have an exact quote for this, but, although the terms for "word" are different, the similarity in Isaiah 11:4 is unmistakable: 'he shall smite the earth with the word (*logo*) of his mouth and with the breath of his lips shall he destroy the ungodly.'"

[281] See Isa 49:3–6.

[282] Gordon Fee, *God's Empowering Presence*, p. 729: "He [Paul] would simply not have understood the fascination with 'words' that one finds among some contemporary charismatics, as though what we speak against the devil is what will defeat him. Paul's aim is higher than that. God has something to say, to be sure, but it is not some ad hoc word directed at Satan. Such an understanding surely endows Satan with far more authority in our present world than this text allows. Rather, as vv. 18–20 confirm, the 'word of God' that is the Spirit's sword is the faithful speaking forth of the gospel in the arena of darkness, so that men and women might hear and be delivered from Satan's grasp."

[283] William Wilder, "The Use (or Abuse) of Power in High Places", p. 190.

[284] It is possible that Paul has in mind a connection to what he mentioned at the end of chapter 4 of the letter, about "getting angry" in a way that is appropriate. Anger on the part of God's community should not be an enduring attitude and, as discussed earlier, should be aroused by and directed at the kinds of things that make God angry. Its objective should be to shine God's light and do something to intervene against the injustice that angers Him.

allowed to flourish; Israel has failed to be the light to the Gentiles showing them the path back to relationship with God, and has neglected to uphold dignity and justice in its own community. God sets things right, establishing righteousness (and so justice) by wearing it as his body armour, and bringing salvation through the wearing of the helmet.[285] Paul encourages God's community to put on these same two pieces of armour, the armour Israel refused to wear, and so to fight the battle against the evil and injustice that undermines humanity and the rest of God's creation.

The last clear parallel to passages found in Isaiah is in Ephesians 6:15, about "feet ready to spread the Good News of Peace". In Isaiah 52:7, the prophet calls on Israel to "wake up"[286] and be "clothed in strength" because evil (represented in this passage by "unclean and godless people") will "no longer enter your gates".[287] Part of this "waking up" is Israel's awareness that God lives up to His name: He is the God who saves.[288] The prophet then describes the "beautiful feet" of those who are on the mountains proclaiming "good news of peace and salvation, the news that the God of Israel reigns!" Paul refers to this as the example of readiness to spread the Good News as God's community battles evil alongside God. The community of God's people knows Who reigns! It understands that God has already defeated the enemy, that victory is certain and that right will prevail; that is the Good News of Peace. Now it is simply a matter of spreading this news to the rest of the world, bringing hope and comfort and courage to those in darkness as well as to one another. The enemy still works his tricks, but the Lord has conquered evil and is in the process of renewing the world;[289] the fate of the enemy is inevitable.[290] It is the continual retelling of the Good News that keeps

---

[285] Paula Qualls and John D. Watts, "Isaiah in Ephesians", p. 254: "… [T]he Lord responds as a divine warrior, wearing righteousness as a breastplate, bringing judgment and salvation and demanding righteousness (v. 17)."

[286] This phrase is of particular interest since Paul has also used it in 5:14, quoting what is thought to be a communal baptismal hymn: "Awake, oh sleeper…"

[287] Isaiah 52:1 (NLT).

[288] Isaiah 12:2, "The LORD God is my strength and song; He has become my salvation" (NLT).

[289] N. T. Wright, *The New Testament and the People of God* (Minneapolis: Fortress, 1992), p. 460: "…[T]he Christians believed that Israel's god, being the creator, would physically recreate those who were his own, at some time and in some space the other side of death. Unlike the Pharisees, they believed that this still-future hope had begun to happen already, in Jesus' resurrection, and that this event served as the prototype for that of others. Paul is again one of the clearest spokesmen for this view, but it is emphasized all over, in John, 1 Peter, Revelation, and elsewhere." In his footnote, Wright references 1 Cor 15:12–28, John 11:25, 1 Pet 1:3–5, and Rev 2:10.

[290] Romans 8:3. "God went for the jugular when he sent his own Son. He didn't deal with the problem as something remote and unimportant. In his Son, Jesus, he personally took on the human condition, entered the disordered mess of struggling humanity in order to set it right once and for all" (The Message).

this reality in view. Interestingly, the word "feet", in addition to suggesting the image of news being carried by messengers, is used to imply that the Good News is the foundation on which God's community stands, and remains standing in spite of all that evil can do; it is from this foothold, fitted with the rest of the armour, that it can confidently wrestle against evil.[291]

The one piece of armour that has no parallel in Isaiah is the "shield of faith". Some believe this may be the one piece of armour for which Paul found an analogy in the traditional outfit of a Roman soldier.[292] The shield was an important part of a Roman soldier's armour, protecting him from attack, especially from arrows. It is not unusual, then, that Paul would use the analogy of the shield with reference to the "fiery arrows" of the evil one to symbolize the protection that faith gives to God's community. Faith is the way to cover oneself from attack. We have already discussed the importance of the term "faith" in Paul's writing as denoting trust or confidence in the person of Christ as the assurance of what God has promised to humanity.[293] This fits with the way Paul started this section of the letter, encouraging God's community to "be strong in the Lord and in the strength of His power". The love and faithfulness of Christ and the power and effectiveness of what He has done are our source of strength; trusting in Him, and in the strength that He gives, acts as a shield to ward off the undermining attack of evil.

Clearly, the ability to wear such armour requires us to be in relationship with the triune community of Father, Son, and Spirit. Since we are part of God's family, His enemy is our enemy. The god we once worshipped while living in darkness[294] is actually the enemy of our true God and King, and of our humanity. This enemy would love to see us fight amongst ourselves, but, as Paul declares,

---

[291] We must keep in mind what was mentioned earlier: the Good News as communicated by the gospel writers is not only that our sins our forgiven, but that Christ is now the true and rightful King over creation. This knowledge makes us aware of the defeat of evil and gives us our identity in relationship to our Lord the King. Our humanity has been redeemed and restored to relationship with the Father, Son, and Spirit. This knowledge can be trusted we are to live it out in its fullness as God's community, participating in God's renewal of all creation.

[292] Frank Gaebelein, ed., *The Expositor's Bible Commentary*, vol. 11, p. 88. Commentator Skevington Wood suggests that the shield of Paul's metaphor could be the "large oblong or oval *scutum* the Roman soldier held in front of him for protection. It consisted of two layers of wood glued together, covered with linen and hide, and bound with iron. Soldiers often fought side by side with a solid wall (*testudo*) of shields. But even a single-handed combatant found himself sufficiently protected. After the siege of Dyrachium, Sceva counted no less than 220 darts sticking into his shield."

[293] See footnote 83.

[294] Ephesians 2:2 echoes here: "You once lived like walking dead people – everything you did betrayed your humanity. You walked by the drum beat of this world and its lead drummer who fills the air with sounds of rebellion for his followers."

that is not where our fight lies; we don't fight against each other. Evil works through our fellow human beings, and our focus should be to fight it rather than them. Paul especially points out that evil works at a cosmic level, behind the powers, authorities, and worldly structures that serve to perpetuate it in society. Nothing indicated this more persuasively than the example of the corruption, greed, and domination of the Roman Empire over the then-known world. The purported "great Republic" was actually a great failure.[295] Roman leaders resorted to violence among themselves to maintain domination and superiority, and the wealthy were so possessed by greed and the pursuit of power that they were prepared to inflict all kinds of misery on the masses. They spoke of "faith" and "keeping their word", but quickly broke faith and their word for selfish gain.[296] They tried to disguise this behind their crafty rhetoric and political patronizing of the common people, but no one was deceived.

Paul lumps together "heads, powers, and world rulers" with "the spiritual forces of evil in the heavens". There is no doubt that the powers of evil lurked behind the violence and injustice perpetrated over the long history of wars between people groups and the conquests celebrated on the walls of Roman buildings. Paul's listeners may have wondered, as we may also wonder, how a small community devoted to God can do battle with such forces. The reality is that the evil behind the big structures of society, behind the movers and shakers, trickles down into the life of every person; the greed of the rulers of the Empire, and the influence of the evil powers behind them, manifested itself in all kinds of evil at street level as well. Paul is encouraging God's community to live out its mandate there, on the street – to be faithful to what it has been called to be and do at the level of relationships in its own sphere of influence, so that the good brought about in those relationships will spread out and up like leaven to other parts of society. And this can actually happen! Luke ends the book of Acts with Paul in prison in Rome, sharing the Good News of Peace with those in Caesar's own household. From the small group of Jewish followers in Judea at the beginning of the book to those serving in Caesar's own house, the news that Christ is King travelled all over the Empire, and it did so by the faithful action of communities devoted to living in relationship with the triune God of grace.

---

[295] It was a failure in terms of upholding any trust in its political leaders to protect the interests of the people of the Empire or take any responsibility for their welfare. The reality was that the wealthy and powerful ended up protecting themselves and their own interests at the expense of the vast majority of the people of the Empire.

[296] Rome will ever go down in history for breaking its promise to the people of Carthage never to invade and subdue them. See Simon Baker, "Revolution", p. 39. Rome took its victories as a sign that the gods favoured its practice of breaking oaths to other peoples and nations.

How did they do this? Well, they were what God called them to be in Christ, living out lives of love and care for their fellow human beings. They showed the love of Christ and the fellowship of the Trinity in their everyday walk. They did not devise schemes to "take down" their oppressors, to wrest power away from them, or to coerce obedience to God's commands; instead they willed peace and harmony toward their fellow human beings, responding with good to whatever evil was doing. This was their offensive weapon; all the other parts of God's armour were for protection, to help God's community withstand the advances and reactions of evil against their being the new humanity. The more we live out our identity in our new humanity and share the Good News of Christ who is the true King, the brighter the light shines and the more the works of darkness are exposed. The enemy hates this, and works against it. But God knows, and equips His people to withstand evil's attack so that His plan to rescue and renew the world prevails.

We are not called to scheme about how to take over the world. That is God's place and not ours; He has already claimed the world through Jesus Christ. The Spirit then works to enact that claim and renew the creation so that it bears God's character and image. As the Psalmist writes so brilliantly:

Why do the nations rage? Why do the people waste their time with futile plans? The kings of the earth prepare for battle; the rulers plot together against the LORD and against his anointed one. "Let us break their chains," they cry, "and free ourselves from this slavery." But the one who rules in heaven laughs. The Lord scoffs at them. Then in anger he rebukes them, terrifying them with his fierce fury. For the LORD declares, "I have placed my chosen King on the throne in Jerusalem, my holy city."[297]

The rulers plot in vain, says the Psalmist; they are wasting their time. It's a done deal. God already has Someone on the throne who will be the world ruler. The way He rules, with truth and righteousness, will transform humanity and creation. He will bring salvation to humanity and instill faith in the hearts of those who receive Him. That faith, that trust in His faithfulness, will become their foundation for living out their life as God desires. All these things are part of God's armour, given to us through Christ, and we are empowered by them through the Spirit.

I know that many believers wonder these days whether God's community should get involved in lobbying governments to promote and protect our values,

---

[297] Psalm 2:1–6 (NLT).

and whether we should take up arms against "evil" nations to prevent further evil.[298] We need to trust that if we live out our lives as God's community with the earnest commitment that Paul outlines in this letter, we will not need to worry so much about lobbying governments and taking up arms. The world will see that we are his disciples by our love,[299] even in the way that we battle evil. If that love eventually won an entire Empire over to pledging allegiance to Christ, then what will that same love do today in our villages, towns, cities, and nations? What would your world look like if the community of God's people that you are part of lived in a perpetual expression of love and care? What would it look like with evil purged from its streets?

What Paul says next is crucial to understanding the long-term impact God's community can have on our world. Having encouraged the readers of his letter to put on God's armour and resist evil alongside Him by living out its calling as His community, Paul reminds them to stay in constant communication with and reliance on God. He asks them to bring their requests to God: whatever is of concern to them as a community they are to submit to God in prayer. They are to bring their prayers for "all the holy ones" as well – not just for themselves and their own local group of believers, but for the whole body of Christ.

These are not just random prayers about the bumps and curves of daily life, as important and significant as those are to each and every member of God's community; rather, Paul is urging God's community to pray that every believer and believing community will be what God has called them to be in the world. The prayer is that as a community they will know the breadth and depth of God's love and express that love continually, toward each other and to the world around them. Paul wants his listeners to pray that God's community will fight evil with good, that they will make use of God's armour trusting that it will help them, and that they will stand firm. The prayer is for God's community to mature in this way, because the thing that will change the world is the community living out its corporate and private life in the way Paul has described throughout chapters 4, 5, and 6. The community's continual posture in prayer is crucial to staying focused, connected to God, and ready to be His community in the world.

Naturally, none of this is possible without the Spirit. Paul mentions that their continual prayer for themselves and others is to be "in the Spirit". Throughout the letter, he has emphasized the Spirit's role in transforming and

---

[298] As we have seen historically, what one nation deems evil, the other proclaims as good. No doubt, at times, the identification of someone or something as evil has been subjective.

[299] John 13:35. "Your love for one another will prove to the world that you are my disciples" (NLT).

empowering God's community to be the new humanity. Prayer is a Spirit-activity:[300] it is God the Spirit who empowers His community to pray. Along with the "sword of the Spirit", our sole weapon of offence which is God's Spirit-empowered word, comes the indwelling presence of that same Spirit within God's community, praying with us so that we can fight effectively and intentionally. Echoes of Romans 8:26–27 ring out at this point: our efforts to pray in keeping with God's purposes may flag, or we may not know how to pray, but the Spirit helps us in our weakness by expressing our plea in a way that transcends words. Paul, in the Romans passage, encourages believers to let the Spirit voice their requests to God the Father in harmony with His intentions in battling evil.[301]

The other important ingredient in all of this is perseverance, and this in turn involves constant vigilance. In his letter Paul is describing a continuous, habitual way of being God's community in the world. Only as that community maintains its character, alertness, and relationship with the Father, Son, and Spirit over time will it have any effectiveness as a participant in God's work of pushing back evil in our world. The ones who stand firm, who carry on through every circumstance, who are fully aware both of the enemy's stratagems and the source of their strength, will be the heroes of the faith; by wearing God's armour and praying in the Spirit, those who "stay awake" and persevere will change the world. God has turned the light on, now we are to keep it on! It will need trimming and refuelling, and will need to be passed on so it can be ignited in others.

Staying close to God will ensure this, as His Spirit does His work on the inside. It will also need our cooperation, even when we don't feel like it. This task goes beyond "feeling like it"; it is a necessity, because so much is at stake. We may find it easy to get off track and lose sight of what we are to be, and even easier just to give up when the going gets tough. In the world Paul inhabited, there was enough cause for discouragement in the plight of everyday people to make

---

[300] Gordon Fee, *God's Empowering Presence*, p. 731: "… [W]hat this text does show is that, unlike most contemporary believers, Paul considered prayer to be above all an activity empowered by the Spirit. It also indicates the crucial role the Spirit plays in our continuing 'warfare' against Satan. For Paul, the concern was not only that they be clothed with the armour that Christ provides in the gospel, but that they take the enemy on by Spirit-empowered proclamation and Spirit-inspired praying."

[301] "And the Holy Spirit helps us in our distress. For we don't even know what we should pray for, nor how we should pray. But the Holy Spirit prays for us with groanings that cannot be expressed in words" (NLT). The context in Romans 8 is our own groaning and that of the rest of creation as we await the transformation that God has promised through Christ, to take place at the end when God's plan is fulfilled and evil is purged from the world.

anyone give up. But Paul is saying, "Don't give up!" It's the "long obedience in the same direction"[302] that will enable us to reach the end.

God has given His community incredible grounds for faith and hope. Having been restored to relationship with Him, it is now time for us to spread the Good News and let everyone else know, and the way to do that is to live the way He has called us to live. God's community is far from fragile; in relationship with the Father, Son, and Spirit, it is the most vital force on earth. Eugene Peterson puts it this way:

> Do you think of Christian faith as a fragile style of life that can flourish only when the weather conditions are just right, or do you see it as a tough perennial that can stick it out through storm and drought, survive the trampling of careless feet and the attacks of vandals? Here is a biblical writer's view: 'He grew up before him like a young plant, and like a root out of dry ground … He was despised and rejected by men; a man of sorrows, and acquainted with grief …. He was oppressed, and he was afflicted.' It is a portrait of extreme rejection and painful persecution. What can come of such a poor, precarious beginning? Not much, it would seem. Yet look at the results: 'He shall see his offspring, he shall prolong his days; the will of the LORD shall prosper in his hand; he shall see the fruit of the travail of his soul and be satisfied; by his knowledge shall the righteous one, my servant, make many to be accounted righteous; and he shall bear their iniquities' (Isa. 53). The person of faith outlasts all the oppressors. Faith lasts.[303]

The resurrection of Christ, alluded to in chapter 1 of Paul's letter, is to be comprehended in terms of the extent of its power working in and through God's community. Paul prays, in verse 19 of that chapter, "I want you to know the immeasurable greatness of His power in His community." The transformative power of what Christ has done for humanity is what God, by His Spirit, puts to work in His community. This power gives Christ all authority to set things right in the world, and Paul says that Christ gives that authority to His church. It is an authority expressed through the community's ability, in Christ, to live

---

[302] I borrow the phrase from the title of the book by Eugene Peterson. Peterson uses the Psalms of Ascent to describe the posture and character of God's community in relationship with God, living out its mandate and hope in a world that speaks and lives the opposite. See Eugene Peterson, *A Long Obedience in the Same Direction* (Downers Grove, IL: Intervarsity Press, 1980).
[303] Ibid., p. 122.

out His life in the world and bring transformation. The world cannot ignore this authority when it is faithfully exercised by the community. No less than a continuous perseverance in doing so is what Paul urges in his letter.

I feel that in our day, we have complicated our identity and calling as a church. There has never been a "busier" church than the North American church today. We are busy with programs, events, strategies of outreach, leadership endeavours, and global initiatives that rival any other organization in our world. The church is making headway on so many fronts in an effort to fulfill Christ's mandate, but at the same time we have lost a lot of ground in the hearts and minds of our neighbours around us. Evil has worked overtime to distract us into being so globally-minded as a community that we have lost interest in loving and caring for those around us. Perhaps this mindset is more typical of the evangelical church than of other Christian traditions, but if so, we evangelicals have lost the important focus on driving back evil by doing good in our very own neighbourhoods. I hear the words of Paul in Romans 13:13, "We should be decent and true in everything we do," calling us to reinstate a culture of honouring humanity by living decently ourselves among our neighbours, always keeping in mind that our actions toward others should reflect what God wills them to be in Christ's new humanity. I fear we have lost an appreciation for the "immeasurable greatness of His power" as it is manifested in this way. But if we look at Jesus' ministry on earth, we see Him doing this very thing – restoring dignity and honour to human life by engaging with others as they will become through His death and resurrection.

If we prove faithful in our own local communities, I believe that we will influence the larger community, because such transformation of society happens at the street level. Change at the street level will eventually effect change at the national and global levels. The church has proved this throughout history in various parts of the world, and we can follow in that tradition of bringing transformation in our own day. It took three short centuries for the church to change an Empire. What could we do in the next three centuries, should King Jesus not return in that time, if we persevere in who He has called us to be?

Chapter Ten

A PERSONAL NOTE

Ephesians 6:19–24

Pray for me that when I open my mouth, words will be given to me so I can make known with confidence the mystery of the Good News of which I am a representative in chains, so that in [those chains] I can speak boldly in the way I should. Tychicus, beloved brother and faithful servant in the Lord, will let you know how I'm doing. I'm sending him to you so that you may know more about how we're doing and he can comfort your hearts [with the news]. Peace to the brothers, and love, with faith from God the Father and the Lord Jesus Christ. Grace be with all who love our Lord Jesus Christ with a genuine love.

A LEADER'S HEART

Paul's final words in the letter of Ephesians give us a glimpse into the heart of this faithful leader. Paul always sees himself as part of God's community. Even though he writes at a geographical distance, his heart is always with the people to whom he is writing. As the kind of leader who not only gives to the community but also grows along with it, Paul asks his listeners to remember to pray for him. Being "in chains", Paul feels more than ever that he has been given an opportunity to share the Good News that can transform those around him. Like any other believer, he needs the community's prayers in the Spirit so that God's will might be accomplished through him in his situation.

Paul never felt disappointed that he had been unable to go to Spain, as he had desired, to continue the work of spreading the Good News there.[304] He was prepared to carry out his commission to preach to the Gentiles wherever God took him. In the book of Acts we see a great resolve on Paul's part to head to Jerusalem after his three missionary journeys, knowing that whatever the details of God's plan for him were, it included getting to Rome; being in Rome was a strategic objective, as it meant an opportunity to influence the entire Empire.

---

[304] This was Paul's aim when he wrote to the believers in Rome. As his situation unfolded, it became clear that God had different plans for him, and that he would make it to Rome only in chains. Whether he would get to Spain or not became a secondary issue by that time.

But in Acts 21, on a trip to Jerusalem to deliver the famine relief money from the churches in Asia Minor, it was prophesied that Paul would be arrested by the Jewish leaders in Jerusalem and taken to Rome as a prisoner. Luke (who was there) remembers Paul's response when the believers in Caesarea begged him not to go on to Jerusalem: "Why all the weeping? You are breaking my heart! For I am ready not only to be jailed in Jerusalem but also to die for the sake of the Lord Jesus."[305]

The rest of the book of Acts chronicles Paul's arrest in Jerusalem and the perilous voyage to Rome after having been held in a Roman prison in Caesarea for two years. In all that time, Paul shared the Good News with two successive ruling Roman governors and their wives,[306] one regional King and his sister,[307] the Captain of the Imperial Regiment[308] that had custody of Paul on the way to Rome, the chief official of the Island of Malta,[309] whose father was healed when Paul prayed for him, and all the inhabitants of the island who witnessed the healing. Paul also shared the Good News with his fellow passengers on the ship to Rome – assuring them, through a vision given him by the Lord, that they would be shipwrecked but everyone would survive – as well as with all the Roman officials who handled his transport from Rhegium in southern Italy to the Three Taverns at the outskirts of Rome, a favourite meeting place for Christians coming in and out of the city.[310]

Luke tells us that, while in Rome, Paul was "permitted to have his own private lodging, though he was guarded by a soldier."[311] This afforded Paul the opportunity to entertain visitors, with whom he also shared the Good News of God's secret plan for the world and of the new humanity brought by Christ through His death, life, resurrection, and ascension. Only God could place Paul in such an advantageous setting, proclaiming Christ King in the very backyard of the Emperor who declared himself king of the world and descendant of the gods. Luke tells us that Paul spent two years this way, and that he "welcomed all who visited him, proclaiming the Kingdom of God with all boldness and teaching about the Lord Jesus Christ. And no one tried to stop him."[312] In view of the fact that Nero, the deranged great-great-grandson of Augustus Caesar, was Emperor

---

[305] Acts 21:13 (NLT).
[306] Felix and his wife Drusilla, and Festus who took over for Felix (Acts 25:24 – 25:1).
[307] King Agrippa and his sister Bernice (Acts 25:13).
[308] His name was Julius (Acts 27:1).
[309] His name was Publius (Acts 28:7).
[310] Acts 28:15.
[311] Acts 18:16 (NLT).
[312] Acts 28:30-31 (NLT).

at the time, it is all the more astounding that Paul had such freedom to speak of Christ and the Good News of His Lordship over humanity.[313] Here is Paul the Apostle working at the street level, telling all who will listen about the Good News of Christ and God's plan for the world; it is no wonder that he asks the hearers of the Ephesian letter to pray in the Spirit that he may continue to have words to share with those who visit him. He was in a difficult situation which was also the most opportune.

While Paul was preaching the Good News of Christ to Nero's servants, family, and fellow leaders, Nero was perpetrating his evil throughout the Empire. Paul was doing battle in Rome against the darkness of that Empire. He needed the support and prayers of God's community and the help of the Spirit so that he could continue being faithful. He needed God's community to persevere with him, knowing the good that God was doing through him among the faithful followers of Christ all over the Empire. This is the heart of a leader, sensitive to the need of others as well as to his own need for them.

Paul's submission to God's plan in his life meant that he was able to engage the hearts of both Jews and Gentiles, sharing with them the Good News of God's grace. There is no doubt that a community would have grown up around Paul in those two years spent under prison guard in Rome. Clusters of believers began to scatter throughout the city, creating more house churches where both Jews and Gentiles gathered to pray and to sing psalms, hymns, and spiritual songs together, giving thanks to God and making music in their heart to the Lord. As they submitted to one other out of reverence for Christ and reached out to their neighbours in love, these faithful followers showed a different humanity in the face of the moral brokenness of Roman society. Those in darkness saw a light in these people who lived out care and compassion, love and acceptance. Many would have been awakened to the light of Christ and joined God's community. Who knows how many carried that light from Rome to distant corners of the Empire, even to Spain!

In the story of Paul we see God's community at work, the Good News being spread through the love for others that comes from being awakened to the light of Christ and empowered by the Spirit. Paul now sends his letter off with Tychicus,

---

[313] Nero became insecure in his position as Emperor, which he had achieved only by virtue of blood line. He lived in the shadow of his great-great-grandfather Augustus and the great feats and conquests that had funded his architectural enhancements of Rome. Nero plundered temple treasuries to lead an ostentatiously lavish existence in Rome, setting himself up visually as the most powerful man in all the Empire. He did away with anyone who rivalled his claim to the throne. See Simon Baker, *Ancient Rome: The Rise and Fall of an Empire* (BBC Books, 2007; EPub file), chapter III, "Nero".

one of the many faithful members of Paul's "ministry team" who helped him by delivering his letters and providing for his needs while in prison. This "beloved brother" would begin circulating the letter throughout the churches in Asia Minor as an update from their spiritual father. Years later the letter landed in our Bible under the name of the Ephesians, the last community to have handled and read it.

In the letter's final words, Paul leaves them with peace, love, and faith – the three things he has spent the entire letter declaring and applying to his listeners' life and community. His hope is that these lovers of Christ will never allow the earnestness and intensity of their love to diminish.[314] Having encountered people who were peddling the Good News for their own gain,[315] Paul was concerned that those who genuinely loved Christ and His community would be encouraged by the letter so that they would continue to be what God had called them to be. These were the ones who "got" what God's community is about. No doubt his hope was that some who were not authentic disciples would, through his letter and through the encouragement of others, also reach the point where they saw the wonder and beauty of God's plan and responded with genuine love for the Lord. Paul wanted above all to see the churches thrive as God's community and live out their calling, so that the Spirit would work through them and transform the world around them. History shows us that those early believers did just that. They poured their lives out as a community, sharing the Good News of Peace with all around them, honouring others and relating to them according to the new humanity given by Christ.

---

[314] Frank E. Gaebelein, ed. *The Expositor's Bible Commentary*, vol. 11. p. 92. Commentator Skevington Wood points out that the phrase *en aphtharsia* has the connotation "unending", but he prefers a translation focusing on its core meaning "in uncorruptness", so that the reference by Paul is to a relationship of love with the Lord Jesus Christ that has no taint of corruption. However, the two qualities may overlap, since only love that is without corruption can be without end: "It could be related to the whole phrase 'all who love our Lord Jesus Christ' and signify that lovers of the Lord are even now guaranteed and indeed enjoy eternal life, i.e., that they love the Lord Jesus Christ as already tasting immortality." I think that, given the context of the whole letter, in which Paul has been encouraging genuine love that is demonstrated through action, "genuineness" is what Paul hopes for now in his goodbye.

[315] We see this in Philippians, where Paul points out that some were peddling the Good News for selfish reasons (Phil 1:17).

CONCLUSION

A great mystery has been revealed to us. The God who resides in the "heavenly places" is our Father who lavishes on us all His Spiritual gifts. For the early believers who came from pagan backgrounds, the "heavenly places" were inhabited by spirits, gods, and magic that played havoc with humanity. Paul takes this language and commandeers it to express the authority and power of God the Father, the Hebrew God spoken of by the prophets, who has made Himself known to humanity through the person of His Son, Jesus Christ. It is this God who gives His own Spirit and solidifies our place and identity in relationship to Him. As an expression of His love and great pleasure, He lavishes on us the gift of community with Him, adopting us into the circle of Father, Son, and Spirit.[316]

This gift transforms our humanity. The work of Christ is applied to us by the Spirit so as to change us from "walking dead people", living in darkness and hostility and following the dark powers of the "heavenlies", into a new, united humanity living in the light of relationship with God through the gift of Christ. This gift restores us to what God designed us to be from the beginning, created to live in a way that brings harmony to the world around us. We are no longer at odds with each other. In Christ, God has made a way for humanity to leave behind its hostile existence and exchange it for one of peace with Him and with others. Together, God has made a way for the human race to become one family again where there is complete and open access to the Father, Son, and Spirit and therefore abundant joy for living. The very life of the Trinity now runs through God's community.

Paul calls this the "new humanity." In the letter of Ephesians he encourages readers to live out this gift of new humanity together as God's community. Forgoing all the connections with darkness, this community now lives in such a way as to redeem all relationships, submitting to one another out of reverence for Christ and using their diverse gifts to build one another up. It is a true reflection on earth of the community of the Trinity in heaven, bearing the image of the triune God to all creation. It lives by the power of the Spirit in the knowledge of life reinterpreted by the Person of Jesus Christ, so that as it does so, the light

---

[316] Gordon Fee, *God's Empowering Presence*, pp. 667–668.

of true humanity in Christ shines on others in the world, pushing back the darkness, exposing evil, and awakening people to the beauty of life lived in relationship with God.

Rather than fear what lurks in the "heavenly places", God's community can now rest assured that in those places King Jesus has taken control and has all authority and power. That authority has also been given to them as God's community, so that together with Christ, wearing God's armour and praying in the Spirit, they can battle evil in the confident knowledge that victory is assured.

Given this big picture, there can be no doubt of the cosmic importance of this letter in the body of literature produced by the Apostle Paul, inspired by God to stand as a living testimony to His desire for all humanity. Having the freedom in this letter to write his large thoughts about what God is up to in our world, Paul pens it as a final "manifesto" of what the Christian community is all about. It exists because of God's express desire to restore humanity to Himself and renew its true nature and identity, imprinted on it by Him from the beginning. It is Christ who has accomplished this and who works in humanity from the inside, by His Spirit, to ensure that God's community becomes what the Father desires.

There is a keen sense in this letter that the end has not come yet. Evil still lurks in the background, trying to keep humanity in the darkness that first overtook it at the fall in Genesis. But the truth is that evil has been conquered and its hold on humanity has been severed. Its power has been diminished. All it has left is the desperate attempt to keep humanity from recognizing who God is. In the face of this, God has raised up His community to peel back the darkness for its blind, sleeping brothers and sisters so that they might awaken to the reality of their lives in relationship with the triune God of grace. The Spirit of God working in God's community effects a revelation of something that has so far been a mystery to humankind; in its darkened heart, humanity felt vestiges of something better than its "walking dead" existence, but had no way of finding it. God, our Father, has revealed it through Christ and is making it known by His Spirit through His community.

The world knows there is something different about humanity since the appearance of Jesus. Thomas Cahill, in his book *Desire of the Everlasting Hills*, asserts that:

[W]hether we are Jew or Christian, believer or atheist, the figure of Jesus – as final Jewish prophet, as innocent and redeeming victim, as ideal human being – is threaded through our society and folded into our imagination in such a way that it cannot be excised. He is the mysterious ingredient that laces everything we taste, the standard by which all moral actions are finally judged.[317]

As the church emerged from the 1st century AD, its influence as a community living in relationship with the triune God of grace impacted the world for the better. These words of Paul in Ephesians resound loudly in the life that the church has lived out over the last 2000 years; the impact is no less than astounding. The society and culture we enjoy owes its existence to the declaration by God's community that true humanity can be lived out with God's help if people give themselves to Christ and let His Spirit work on the inside to renew their hearts and minds and make them the masterpiece that God intended.

But the darkness remains, and the enemy does not give up. More than ever before, as God's community, we need to carry on spreading the Good News of Peace so that we do not forget where we have come from and so that we help others realize who they are in Christ. We have so many brothers and sisters who live in the darkness of their old humanity and need a way out. That way out becomes visible as God's community faithfully and prayerfully perseveres in living out its life as the new humanity. I pray that, having read this book, you too have a greater resolve to live out your true humanity in relationship to God and His community in a way that builds that community up – so that it continues to be the entity on earth that pushes back evil with good and peels back the darkness in the lives of others, making way for the light and love of Christ to enfold them into relationship with the Father, Son, and Spirit.

---

[317] Thomas Cahill, *Desire of the Everlasting Hills: The World Before and After Jesus* (New York: Nan A. Talese, 1999), p. 319. Cahill in particular has decided to tell history through "the narratives of grace": "the recounting of those blessed and inexplicable moments when someone did something for someone else, saved a life, bestowed a gift, gave something beyond what was required in the circumstance." As for Christianity, Cahill believes that it has forever influenced and changed the Western world.

WORKS CITED

Aland, Kurt. *The Greek New Testament*. New York: United Bible Societies, 1983.

Arndt, William, F., Wilbur Gingrich, Frederick W. Danker, and Walter Bauer. *A Greek-English Lexicon of the New Testament and Other Early Christian Literature: A Translation and Adaptation of the Fourth Revised and Augmented Edition of Walter Bauer's Griechisch-deutsches Wörterbuch Zu Den Schriften Des Neuen Testaments Und Der Übrigen Urchristlichen Literatur*. Chicago: University of Chicago, 1979.

Bailey, Kenneth E. *Paul Through Mediterranean Eyes: Cultural Studies in 1 Corinthians*. Downers Grove: IVP Academic, 2011.

Baker, Simon. *Ancient Rome: The Rise and Fall of an Empire*. BBC Books, 2007. EPub File.

Barth, Karl, and Edwyn Clement Hoskyns. *The Epistle to the Romans*. London: Oxford University Press, 1968.

Bauckham, Richard J. *Jesus: A Very Short Introduction*. Oxford: Oxford University Press, 2011.

Bradley, K. R. *Slaves and Masters in the Roman Empire: A Study in Social Control*. New York: Oxford University Press, 1987.

Brown, Colin. *The New International Dictionary of New Testament Theology*, vol. 1. Grand Rapids, MI: Zondervan, 1975.

Bruce, F. F. *The Epistles to the Colossians, to Philemon, and to the Ephesians*. Grand Rapids, MI: Eerdmans, 1984.

Cahill, Thomas. *Desire of the Everlasting Hills: The World before and after Jesus*. New York: Nan A. Talese, 1999.

Caird, G. B. *Paul's Letters from Prison: Ephesians, Philippians, Colossians, Philemon, in the Revised Standard Version*. Oxford: Oxford University Press, 1976.

Calvin, John. *Institutes of the Christian Religion*. Translated by Henry Beveridge. Grand Rapids, MI: Eerdmans, 1953.

Durant, Will. *Caesar and Christ: A History of Roman Civilization and of Christianity from Their Beginnings to A.D. 325*. New York: Simon and Schuster, 1972.

Fee, Gordon D. *God's Empowering Presence: The Holy Spirit in the Letters of Paul*. Peabody, MA: Hendrickson, 1994.

Fee, Gordon D., and Douglas K. Stuart. *How to Read the Bible Book by Book: A Guided Tour*. Grand Rapids, MI: Zondervan, 2002.

Gaebelein, Frank E., ed. *The Expositor's Bible Commentary: With the New International Version of the Holy Bible, Ephesians through Philemon*. Grand Rapids, MI: Zondervan, 1981.

Glancy, Jennifer A. *Slavery in Early Christianity*. Minneapolis: Fortress Press, 2006.

Goodman, Martin. *The Roman World: 44 BC – 180 AD*. Routledge, 2002.

Gudorf, Michael E. "The Use of Pale in Ephesians 6:12." *Journal of Biblical Literature* 117.2 (Summer 1998): 331–35.

Gundry, Robert H. *Commentary on Ephesians*. Grand Rapids: Baker Academic, 2010. EPub File.

Gunton, Colin E. *The Christian Faith: An Introduction to Christian Doctrine*. Oxford, UK: Blackwell, 2002.

Hendriksen, William. *Galatians and Ephesians*. Grand Rapids, MI: Baker, 1979.

Herrington, Jim, R. Robert Creech, and Trisha Taylor. *The Leader's Journey: Accepting the Call to Personal and Congregational Transformation*. San Francisco: Jossey-Bass, 2003.

Hiebert, D. Edmond. "God's Creative Masterpiece." *Direction* 23.1 (Spring 1994): 116–24.

Holy Bible: New Living Translation. Wheaton, IL: Tyndale House, 1996.

Horsley, Richard A. *Paul and Empire: Religion and Power in Roman Imperial Society*. Harrisburg, PA: Trinity International, 1997.

Jeffers, James S. *The Greco-Roman World of the New Testament Era: Exploring the Background of Early Christianity*. Downers Grove, IL: InterVarsity, 1999.

Kraemer, Ross Shepard, and Mary Rose D'Angelo. *Women and Christian Origins*. Oxford University Press, 1999. EPub File.

Kruger, C. Baxter. *The Great Dance: The Christian Vision Revisited*. Vancouver: Regent College Publishing, 2005.

Lane, Eugene, ed. *Cybele, Attis, and Related Cults: Essays in Memory of M. J. Vermaseren.* Leiden: E.J. Brill, 1996.

Layman, Fred D. "Male Headship in Paul's Thought." *Wesleyan Theological Journal* 15:1 (Spring 1980): 46–67.

McKnight, Scot. *The King Jesus Gospel: The Original Good News Revisited.* Grand Rapids, MI: Zondervan, 2011.

Miller, J. David. "Translating Paul's Words about Women." *Stone-Campbell Journal* 12:Spring (2009): 61–71.

Moulton, H. K. *The Analytical Greek Lexicon Revised.* Grand Rapids, MI: Zondervan, 1978.

Peterson, Eugene H. *A Long Obedience in the Same Direction: Discipleship in an Instant Society.* Downers Grove, IL: InterVarsity, 1980.

————. *The Message: The Bible in Contemporary Language.* Colorado Springs: NavPress, 2002.

Polhill, John B. *Paul and His Letters.* Nashville, TN: Broadman & Holman, 1999.

Qualls, Paula, and John D. W. Watts. "Isaiah in Ephesians." *Review and Expositor* 93 (1996): 249–59.

Romanello, Stefano. *Lettera Agli Efesini: Nuova Versione, Introduzione E Commento.* Milano: Paoline, 2003.

Stark, Rodney. *Cities of God: The Real Story of How Christianity Became an Urban Movement and Conquered Rome.* San Francisco: HarperOne, 2006.

————. *The Rise of Christianity: How the Obscure, Marginal Jesus Movement Became the Dominant Religious Force in the Western World in a Few Centuries.* San Francisco: HarperOne, 1997.

————. *The Triumph of Christianity: How the Jesus Movement Became the World's Largest Religion.* New York: HarperOne, 2011.

————. *The Victory of Reason: How Christianity Led to Freedom, Capitalism, and Western Success.* New York: Random House, 2005.

Stott, John R. W. *The Message of Ephesians: The Bible Speaks Today.* Downers Grove, IL: Intervarsity, 1979.

Stott, John R. W. *The Spirit, the Church, and the World*. Downers Grove, IL: InterVarsity, 1990.

Suetonius. *The Twelve Caesars*. Harmondsworth, Middlesex: Penguin, 1957.

Suh, Robert. "The Use of Ezekiel 37 in Ephesians 2." *Journal of the Evangelical Theological Society* (December, 2007): 715–33.

Wilder, William N. "The Use (or Abuse) of Power in High Places: Gifts Given and Received in Isaiah, Psalm 68, and Ephesians 4:8." *Bulletin for Biblical Research* 20:2 (2010): 185–200.

Winters, Jeffrey A. *Oligarchy*. Cambridge University Press, 2011. EPub File.

Wright, N. T. *After You Believe: Why Christian Character Matters*. San Francisco: Harper Collins, 2010. EPub File.

———. *How God Became King: The Forgotten Story of the Gospels*. New York: HarperOne, 2012.

———. *Justification: God's Plan & Paul's Vision*. Downers Grove, IL: IVP Academic, 2009.

———. *Paul for Everyone: The Prison Letters: Ephesians, Philippians, Colossians*. Louisville, KY: Westminster John Knox Press, 2004. EPub File.

———. *Simply Jesus: Who He Was, What He Did, Why It Matters*. New York: HarperOne, 2011.

———. *The Challenge of Jesus: Rediscovering Who Jesus Was and Is*. Downers Grove, IL: InterVarsity, 1999.

———. *The Kingdom New Testament: A Contemporary Translation*. New York: HarperOne, 2011.

———. *The New Testament and the People of God*. Minneapolis: Fortress Press, 1992.

———. Chapel Message at the Wheaton Theology Conference, Wheaton College, Chicago, April 16, 2010.

www.ingramcontent.com/pod-product-compliance
Lightning Source LLC
Chambersburg PA
CBHW052341090426
42740CB00028B/2793